January 2016

Circling the Earth
in a Wheelchair

Stan Morse

Stan Morse

Note for Librarians: A cataloguing record for this book is available from Library and Archives Canada at www.collectionscanada.ca/amicus/index-e.html
ISBN 1-4120-5996-8

♻ green power

Printed in Victoria, BC, Canada. Printed on paper with minimum 30% recycled fibre. Trafford's print shop runs on "green energy" from solar, wind and other environmentally-friendly power sources.

TRAFFORD
PUBLISHING™

Offices in Canada, USA, Ireland and UK
This book was published *on-demand* in cooperation with Trafford Publishing. On-demand publishing is a unique process and service of making a book available for retail sale to the public taking advantage of on-demand manufacturing and Internet marketing. On-demand publishing includes promotions, retail sales, manufacturing, order fulfilment, accounting and collecting royalties on behalf of the author.

Book sales for North America and international:
Trafford Publishing, 6E–2333 Government St.,
Victoria, BC v8t 4p4 CANADA
phone 250 383 6864 (toll-free 1 888 232 4444)
fax 250 383 6804; email to orders@trafford.com
Book sales in Europe:
Trafford Publishing (uk) Ltd., Enterprise House, Wistaston Road Business Centre,
Wistaston Road, Crewe, Cheshire cw2 7rp UNITED KINGDOM
phone 01270 251 396 (local rate 0845 230 9601)
facsimile 01270 254 983; orders.uk@trafford.com
Order online at:
trafford.com/05-0897

10 9 8 7 6 5 4 3

Forward

THIS JOURNEY ACTUALLY BEGAN ON THE LAST DAY OF 1971, when my brother and I went skiing at Mission Ridge. On that crisp New Year's Eve morning we drove the forty-five miles to the hill in a 1960 Buick, the last of its era to have tail fins. We had gone skiing the previous week, stayed until dark, and on the drive home I nearly fell asleep and ran off the road. I was determined to not make the same mistake twice. We would quit early and be home in time for dinner.

We hit the slopes shortly after nine. The snow was so cold that it squeaked as we came off the top end of the chair and glided off on our first run. The sky was pure blue, wind-whipped crystals bearded the firs and pines, the moguled trails were packed with holiday skiers, I was seventeen and the world was perfectly grand.

Ken preferred the slower and safer paths so we split up after a couple of easy runs. I took the chairlift to the very top of the mountain and on the way up met a Seattle businessman, also an advanced skier. We decided to ski together.

Around eleven-thirty, on what would be the last run of my life, he accidentally crashed into me from behind. I still remember the impact of him colliding hard with my back left side. I saw, from the corner of my eye, part of an arm, a shoulder. I was slammed forward and out of control.

I do not remember hitting the ground or the trees they say I went into. I do not remember them pulling me out of the deep snow bank and rolling me onto my back.

I regained consciousness a few minutes later, swimming up through a crushing pain that was exploding between my shoulder blades and beside my heart. Every shallow breath I struggled to take felt like a grenade going off in my chest. I was taking tiny sips of air, fighting for my life. I begged the ski patrolman to get me off the mountain, told him over and over that I needed to go to a hospital, to see a doctor. Then I blacked out. Years later I learned that they thought I was in the process of dying on that toboggan ride to the waiting ambulance. But the ski patrol got me off the ski hill alive and the paramedics managed to get me to the Deaconess Hospital in Wenatchee.

I spent the first two days heavily sedated. When the bleeding around my spine finally stopped and my condition was stable, I was put into an ambulance for the three-hour ride across the mountains to the University of Washington Hospital in Seattle.

The second day in Seattle a blood clot formed in my left leg and it swelled up like a balloon. I already had a permanent IV needle in my arm for hydration and painkillers. To this mix they now added the blood thinner Heparin, hoping to slowly dissolve the clot and relieve the pressure and prevent it from breaking free and moving into my lungs or brain.

A deep bruise inside my right thigh, which had gone undetected, suddenly began dumping my thinned blood into the surrounding tissue. My right leg now swelled as large as my left and produced another life-threatening condition the treatment for which was exactly the opposite as the treatment for the blood clot.

I now had spinal cord damage and paralysis, a blood clot in my left leg, and internal bleeding in my right leg. It was too much trauma even for an athletic seventeen-year-old boy. My body went into shock and my temperature began to climb. That evening it reached 104 degrees, and I was suddenly surrounded by nurses and doctors packing flat ice bags (I distinctly remember they called them *flounders*) against my body to force my temperature down. The neurosurgeon phoned my mother and told her they didn't expect me to make it through to the morning.

I was more durable and stubborn than they had imagined.

I left the hospital four months later in a shiny chrome wheelchair, thankful that I at least had the use of my hands and upper body. I had met several young men on the ward who weren't so lucky. That was the first great lesson of being paralyzed: What you *have* is far more important than what you *lack*.

Mom and Dad were divorced and neither had money. Both had only graduated from high school. Dad seemed to have written off any real future for me. He only visited me in the hospital a few times and I always saw the pain in his face at the realization that his oldest son would be permanently on wheels.

My mother believed in me and offered nothing but encouragement. But she came from a generation where people in wheelchairs were never expected to live normal lives. She believed I could go to college and at least earn my own way in the world. But even she would be amazed by what I would eventually accomplish in my personal and professional lives.

The stereotype of the cripple dies very, very hard.

When I looked around to consider my educational and other options I now faced the future without any meaningful role models to learn from. The Vietnam War was providing a steady stream of wheelchair-bound young men, but the only visible ones were those who appeared on TV in anti-war marches, or in hospital wards as human-interest stories at the end of the evening news. Hardly what a teenage boy wants to be identified with when he's considering how to ask a girl for a date, or trying to figure out how to dance without looking or feeling the fool. Our late President Franklin Delano Roosevelt had sometimes used a chair, but he had also worked hard to conceal this fact.

The few other wheelchair-bound people I knew of had MS, CP or similar degenerative conditions. Unlike them, I could expect to live a normal life span. I believed I could succeed in life despite my disability. But the question was: *How?* The answer was a tough one. I'd have to create a new role model. To do that, I'd need a good job. And for that, I'd need all the education I could get.

I left the hospital on April 30th and enrolled at the local junior college in early June of 1972. Two years later I moved on to Central Washington State College and lived away from home for the first time in my life. After completing my bachelor's degree, I entered law school in the Midwest.

College campus environments proved to be friendly. A few girls were willing to explore dating a guy in a chair. And most students were slow to stereotype someone as incapable merely because he couldn't walk. For those who were unable to accept my condition and include me in their activities, I learned tolerance.

Beyond the college environment, improvements were occurring that would affect my ability to enter the "normal" world. New laws were being enacted to require handicapped access to public places. Airlines no longer insisted that you have someone accompany you on a flight. The concept of *political correctness* was slowly re-orienting people's attitudes toward the less advantaged. Or at least so it seemed.

Life held a fair amount of promise.

I graduated from law school in the spring of 1979 and returned to central Washington to begin my practice. And here came the real world again, right up in my face.

I'll be honest and fair. People try exceptionally hard to be kind. They go out of their way to be nice. But for the most part, they fear the wheelchair and, even more, the reason why you are in it. Perhaps they subconsciously think *it might happen to me or to someone I love.* For the most part, they simply don't know how to relate. The answer is simple: *You relate to someone in a wheelchair as you would to anybody else.* You treat someone in a wheelchair as a person. It really is that simple.

The reality that I was still looked upon as different was driven home when I moved to Seattle in 1983. I couldn't find a job with a law firm, even after filling out applications with practically every firm in the city. A friend who worked at one of the mid-sized downtown firms came to me one day and confessed that I hadn't been hired because I didn't fit their image. He was ashamed, embarrassed; and I'm still proud to have accepted this revelation with some degree of grace. But it opened my eyes. Discrimination might not be politically correct, but it was still the norm.

One year later I found an office-sharing arrangement that eventually worked out just fine. And here I am, fifteen years later, on the verge of traveling and writing, both early loves in my life that seemed, for years, an impossibility. A bit of serendipity, perhaps, that the money and time have come together to make this adventure a possibility. But persistence also played a huge role.

I still have difficulty finding a date. I seldom get invited to parties. No one ever asks if I'd like to come and watch a softball game or go swimming. Many are impressed when they learn that I can drive a car, even though it's the easiest of things to do. Most assume someone comes in to do my housework, my gardening, the daily chores that make up most of our lives. I do all of these routine activities by myself. I always have.

There's a saying about writing fiction that applies equally to what I want to accomplish in this book: *Don't tell, SHOW!* When you write, put your reader into your character's shoes and let them get involved in the story. Let your reader become involved in the story through the eyes of the main character. I now realize the same wisdom is true about being disabled. When I tell people I'm normal, they simply don't believe it. *How can he be? He's in a wheelchair.*

So this story is a comfortable and safe way to see what it's really like to be me, to be in a wheelchair. I'll show you my world. And more than that, I'll give you a grand adventure as part of the bargain.

Half a year on the road is no small commitment, even for someone who can walk. I don't approach this trip without fear and doubt. But it's the best way to make my point. Perhaps the only way.

Day after tomorrow, I leave.

OCTOBER 27

Coast Starlight Train

A COLD SEATTLE RAIN IS MISTING DOWN AS MY FRIEND LARON parks her car at the King Street train station. She lugs my two bags from the trunk and patiently holds them while I put the wheels on my wheelchair and swing into it from the passenger seat.

"Let me take one of those." I reach out expectantly.

"You'll be carting them around for six months." Laron purses her lips, resisting my stubbornness. The delivery of me to the train is her final gift, her last chance at being a part of my adventure. I relent.

A damp draft hinting of pipe tobacco and diesel swirls around us as we pass through the art deco doors. We cross the worn tile, past an empty hollow where the escalator was torn out. Faded posters touting rail travel are taped to the concrete walls. Arthritic loneliness radiates from every corner, every dark hairline crack in the cement.

She sets my suitcase and knapsack on two empty chairs. She's already late for work.

"Is there anything you need? Can I help in some other way?"

"No. I'll be fine."

She gives me a hug, wishes me luck. Leaves. And I hunker down to wait.

I was here once before, nine years ago, to put my mom on the train to L.A. That event now seems forever in the past. My mother, too, is long gone, dead in a car accident in 1993. I suddenly feel lonely and scared, like being three years old and having lost my favorite blanket. I take a deep breath, close my eyes. The moment passes.

As the time for the train's arrival nears the empty spaces gradually fill with clutches of people who form between the rows of worn chairs, competing to be heard in the vaulted hall. Conversations become urgent as the *Coast Starlight* eases in on the tracks outside.

"… no, just to Bakersfield."

"… she won't, till Christmas."

"You kids get over here!"

I look around and see that we're quite an eclectic collection gathered together for the railroad experience: Two Mennonite couples, the men in brimmed black hats and black suits, with long gray beards, their wives in shawls and dresses. A pair of well-dressed, middle-aged gay men, openly affectionate, shepherding four large tooled-leather suitcases. Three teenagers with backpacks. A frail, bent, gray-haired woman huddled tearfully with her daughter and grandchildren. Two men and a woman with only cardboard boxes and plastic bags for luggage, already looking tired at the prospect of thirty-one hours to L.A. in coach seats. A few dozen others. And me, the guy in the wheelchair that children discover with saucer stares.

A couple—young, attractive, dejected—comes toward me from the baggage claim desk. She sits two seats away; he continues to stand, speaking with an Amtrak agent. A piece of luggage has vanished. He tersely describes the contents.

"A video camera. Cookware. Books."

"We'll put a trace on it," the agent says confidently. The husband shrugs in hopelessness.

I ask her where they're coming from and learn they're just off the

Empire Builder from Chicago, headed to Alaska.

"How long are you staying?"

"Two years."

"Are you from Chicago?"

"No, Philadelphia."

"Why Alaska?"

"He got a job." She struggles to smile. Her wedding ring glints of new gold and the small diamond flashes. She sighs and turns to listen to her husband and the agent.

A little girl skips by, twirls toward the platform, entranced by the train. Outside, the newly arrived search anxiously through luggage piled on carts. Duffels, suitcases and boxes quickly disappear. When the last piece is gone the carts are pulled away, clearing the path to the train.

Tension builds. People now glance frequently toward the check-in counter, seeking some clue that boarding is starting.

My gut churns. Is this a colossal mistake? A grandiose delusion? Who will want to read about a guy in a wheelchair going around the world alone? What on God's fine earth has possessed me to abandon the security of a comfortable law practice? I remind myself that I'm escaping winter for an adventure that few have the opportunity to take. *Just cool it. Be calm. This will pass. You'll be okay.*

To distract myself, I check luggage zippers and straps for the umpteenth time. Then I lean down and examine each of the nuts and bolts in my chariot. She was rebuilt this past month; after fifteen years of daily use the paint had become chipped, the bearings encrusted, three spokes were broken out. So she got glossy black enamel, new upholstery and chrome-alloy hardware. I finger each lock nut and they all feel snug.

As I sit back up, a voice bellows from the tinny speakers. "Passengers for the *Coast Starlight* may now check in for boarding."

Two long queues form and the jostling ritual of boarding is finally underway. The woman and I exchange perfunctory wishes for luck.

Another moment of terror congeals as I join the line. Should I turn around and go home? Maybe I won't make it back! I don't even have a Last Will and Testament drawn up! What would it feel like in the last seconds of life to realize I'll never again see my beloved Cascade Mountains? The house where I grew up and now live? What if I get sick? What if I'm injured? *I'm not on the train yet! It's still not too late!*

The line seems to melt in front of me. A man with graying temples looks down placidly, almost bored, from behind the brown Formica counter.

"Sir? Are you able to walk?"

My terror vanishes with his dumb question. Isn't the answer obvious? But twenty-six years as a paraplegic has taught me not to give a smart-aleck reply or to be angry. People just don't know. The condition is so alien; unfathomable to most; a boogey best pushed away to some dark corner of the mind. The number of active people in wheelchairs is tiny and we have such different capabilities. I recall the people I've seen in wheelchairs who have the ability to walk and choose not to. And then there are those who need assistance even to breathe. Such a menagerie we are, truly. How difficult it is for anyone who is "normal" to get any kind of grasp upon what it must be like because "it" is so different from person to person.

"No," I reply. And now any doubt I had about getting on the train is gone. I remember why I'm here, to prove a point, to be an example, to show people like the guy behind the counter that I, too, can do the normal things like taking a train trip even if I can't skip down the aisles.

"You'll have to stay in your cabin," he apologizes. "The diner and lounge cars are upstairs. There's no lift and we can't carry you. But the porter will bring your meals and take care of your other needs." He hands me a boarding pass. I bite my lip and accept it in silence.

I've never traveled by train in the U.S. The booking agent said it would be handicapped accessible, a grab-bag term of infinite variation. I would have loved to visit with other travelers in the lounge car. But what can I do? Nothing.

Concessions are a part of this life. It's usually small things, like having to take my chair apart to get into a car. People comment, "That's sure a lot of work!" as I pop the wheels off and lift them into the back seat.

"What's the alternative?" I reply, always trying to sound upbeat.

You can be philosophical or you can be cynical. Cynicism loses way too many friends.

I'm told to go to car *H* and wait for a conductor. With my dark-green canvas suitcase in my lap and a gray-green backpack slung on the back of my chair, I cruise down the platform to the eighth coach behind the locomotive. A sixty-something couple stands on the black asphalt near the H-coach's doorway, he to smoke, she to be with him. I smile at them and they smile back.

"Where are you going?" he asks.

"L.A."

"Uh, if you don't mind my asking, how come you're in that condition?" Very polite and concerned, but unwilling to say *wheelchair*, as if the word is too harsh.

I puzzled for years about why people ask this question. It's often the first thing they want to know, after introductions. But what difference would it make if it were a birth defect, a car accident, or snow skiing? Why not just accept it and move on to getting to know the person? Someone recently provided the answer with an off-the-cuff remark: "I just want to know it wasn't easy!" When I told him it happened while snow skiing, he flinched. "I ski," was his only comment. So that's it! People want to believe it can't happen to them. That's why they often follow up with, "Well, that sure was a freak accident!" Because *freak* accidents don't happen to *you*. Plain old accidents, conversely, do happen to almost everyone sooner or later. People want confirmation that this terrible thing is so rare that it can't be a possibility in their future. In reality, all accidents are freak occurrences; if they weren't, we wouldn't call them accidents. And to deny the possibility that a disabling accident might be in your future is to ignore a basic premise of life: There are no guarantees. Just possibilities.

I've toyed with saying that I tripped on a crack in the sidewalk, but I've never had the nerve. Besides, I'm happy to have a chance to spread the message that life has charms and pleasures, even if you can't walk.

His face wrinkles with distress and pity. I hate this look.

He senses it and tries to empathize.

"I had a heart attack in August. And my wife, she's color blind all her life." I can't see the woman's eyes behind her sunglasses, and I seriously doubt you can tell by looking at them. I return the husband's grim smile with one of my own.

"Hmmm. That's tough."

What I want to say is that we aren't partners in the same Club of Suffering. I want to tell him of my trip, to prove how capable I am, to show how adventurous, how free, how thrilled I am with being alive. I want to say he's probably more limited by his heart condition than I am by my paralysis. But would I convince him? Or would it just sound like some kind of bogus defensiveness? I remind myself that you cannot *tell* someone a thing this important and expect them to understand. And I've yet to do anything I can *show* to prove my point. I'm not even on the train, the first leg of my journey.

He continues with admiration. "You just hang in there, don't you?" And by now a correction seems pointless.

"Yep. You just keep on moving."

He seems satisfied and takes a thoughtful drag on his cigarette.

"I love the train," the wife says, shifting from the uncomfortable subject. "We travel a lot."

He nods, and then adds, "We used to book the roomettes, but now, we go full-cabin. No use leaving the money for the kids!"

They laugh.

The conductor arrives. "You folks ready to come aboard?"

The husband tosses his cigarette beneath the train and steps up. "See you around," he says, climbing the spiral staircase to the upper deck with his wife close behind.

Larry, the conductor, takes me down a short hall to a room that fills the end of the car, with windows on both sides. There's plenty of space to turn my chair around in. A small stainless-steel sink occupies one corner, a toilet occupies another. Across from these, two opposing seats fill the port side.

I spot a power outlet. "Can I plug my computer in there?"

"Sure."

This makes me feel better about being alone. At least I'll get a lot of writing done.

"Just let me know if there's anything else you need."

"What about showering?"

"Well, there's a shower out in the hall. We can look at it later. I've got to get the other passengers settled right now." He does not sound enthused.

As I unpack my toilet kit and set up my computer the diesel engine hums to life and we move, slow and smooth, from the station. I get a silly grin on my face. I've done it! I sit back, take a deep breath, a chill runs down my spine.

We slide through the rail yard and pick up speed. Seattle's skyscrapers fade into the low-hanging gray clouds. The sheet metal warehouses, the lumberyards, the stockpiles of brick and iron and gravel, gradually disappear.

Within minutes we are easing at fifty through a shallow valley, past row crops, pastures with grazing horses and cattle, farmhouses and barns. Brush and new-growth fir choke the land. Red vine maple invades the railroad right-of-way. Leaves form a thick brown mat in the rail bed ditch. Autumn is slowly pushing the land gray and flat.

Travel brings a sharp awareness, a rediscovered fascination with common things. Water drops and dirt specks on the window glass. Peeling paint on buildings. The silver sheen mirroring a puddle's surface. The red cleft in a blackbird's wing.

After lunch, punctually delivered by Larry the porter, I take stock of my emotions: happy for having started; peeved about the shower, which at a glance I saw was not accessible; and still a little scared about being gone for so long. I also feel the weight of my writing obligations. Will the newspaper articles meet the editor's expectations? What shape will the book take? Writing a book still seems a great mystery. What makes for an interesting read?

A writer with many novels already published once told me, "Keep your day job; it's too hard to make a living at writing." I followed his advice for fourteen years. But I got so tired of lawyer argument, posturing, lawyer jokes, trying to keep clients happy, and the grind of chalking up billable hours. Now, here I am on a train, heading off into the unknown.

My silly grin returns.

An hour later we stop in Tacoma, where passengers hurry off for a quick smoke. They stand in the cold, puffing vigorously, collars pulled high against the late autumn cold, hands stuffed in pockets. After ten minutes the conductor yells "Board!" and the butts are crushed under heel.

New passengers, and the people who brought them to the station, embrace, kiss, shake hands, wipe away reluctant tears. "Goodbye," "Take care!" "I love you!" "Say 'hi' to Grandma." The platform clears; the train doors slam and seal. We glide away.

We're in Portland by mid-afternoon. The sun cuts sharp shadows through the rolling stock and warehouses, rendering the industrial corridor almost black-and-white. A few scutty clouds lie like ragged dumplings against the western horizon.

Portland conjures up for me the image of bridges, everywhere bridges, spanning the river, criss-crossing the rail yard, a tangle of gray concrete ramps and khaki girders. I never fail to get lost when I drive in this city. I stray across the wrong bridge, end up taking the wrong overpass, trying to decipher sudden road signs and return to the safety of Interstate 5. I miss my exit and end up on the wrong side of the river. Were the bridges operated under a toll system I'd spend a small fortune trying to escape from Portland. I'm now happy to be on the train, cutting a linear path through this city of bridges and jumbled highways.

We lumber through the warehouse district, the wheels *kalumphing* at the highway crossings. I begin to think ahead, wondering what Honolulu will bring. Will I find a ship to Australia?

I'm scheduled to dive on the Great Barrier Reef in five weeks, but between now and then I have no definite plans, except to seek out adventure where I can find it. I want a freighter, not a cruise ship, to take me to Australia. I've made a few calls, but had no success. The common response has been, "It's a working ship, and there's too much danger to someone in a wheelchair." But it's precisely the danger I want. Will I find an adventuresome captain who will take me on?

I set this thought aside. Things have a way of taking care of themselves. I must focus upon enjoying the present moment. Because if I start to worry about every possible problem, fear will consume me.

South of Portland the train arrows across the rich bottomland of the Willamette Valley. The grass is still green; horses and cattle graze in fenced pastures; hardy row crops await the final harvest. We motor through Salem, Albany, Eugene, Chemult and Klamath Falls; typical western towns with sleepy streets lined with long-bed pickups and boaty old Buicks, Plymouths and Fords. Men outside the feed stores or the taverns are likely to be wearing cowboy hats or baseball caps with farm supply logos. High school football and basketball games fill up their weekends. The neighbors know each other and are likely to have grown up through Sunday school and Cub Scouts and FFA and church potlucks. We slice past their galvanized steel silos and weathered wooden loading docks with no more warning than a blast from the engine's horn.

Late in the day we leave the level farm country. The engine holds well below its top speed of sixty-nine as the track winds up into the Siskiyou foothills. The leisure of our progress should have the charm of a slow massage. But as a storybook sunset hurls orange wisps against a blue sky, I tire of writing. I'm bored. Jet travel has trained me to expect a quick change of scenery. It's hard to slow down.

Dinner offers only a brief distraction. After Larry has taken away the tray, I peek out through the blue knit curtains and discover that a blackboard darkness has descended upon the day. I pull the curtains tight, shutting out the night, and imagine how nice tomorrow's sun will look cresting the white peaks of the Sierras.

And then I notice something strange. Gliding smoothly along with the curtains drawn I've lost the sense of which direction we are moving. I know, of course, where the locomotive is. I know what direction the train must be headed. But encased in this massive insulating bulk of steel it's hard to detect the small changes in speed, the rush of air, the rise and fall of outside noises, all of the clues that reveal what direction the train is moving. And then, like a wondrous flash of *deja vu*, I realize that the train is a metaphor for my life. On a night train, with the outside world gone dark, one has a hard time perceiving direction. And isn't this just like life? Where without frequent words of encouragement, confirming smiles, an occasional helping hand or a kind suggestion, you can't be certain that you are making progress, maturing, becoming of more value to others. Too many people live their lives like night trains. They build up momentum and forget to check what direction they are headed. Many never realize that you can get off; it just takes some imagination, a little effort. And how many of us care enough to reach out and help people with limited vision to see a better way?

Larry comes to make up my bed, efficiently folding the seats down and arranging cushions, sheets, and blankets. The finished product looks awfully narrow. Do people ever fall out? The tracks outside now fold tightly against the steep contour of the mountains. The train frequently sways from side to side almost violently.

I crave being gently rocked to sleep by the rhythm of the rails, but the undercarriage is squealing and groaning as we curve along a stream-bed and the engine fights to gain altitude. I might as well be riding out an earthquake. Without control of my leg and gut muscles for balance, I have to use my arms to keep from being tossed around, and that gets old, fast.

Then I realize how easily a negative attitude has crept in. I'm being weak. It's time to toughen up.

Fighting for purchase on the tilting floor, I brush my teeth at the tiny sink, pop out my contact lenses, undress, get out of my wheelchair, and slide my legs under the reassuringly tight covers of the single bed. I wedge my chair against the wall with my shoes so that it can't roam around like a drunken sailor.

When I'm finally tucked in, I'm surprised to discover how stable I now feel. The movements of the train, which in my chair were almost dangerous, have become soothing and gentle, almost maternal. The train ambles through the mountains and I sleep like a penny at the bottom of a well.

A Night at LAX

I AWAKEN NOT TO WHITE-PEAKED MOUNTAINS BUT TO HEDGEROW hills lumping the eastern horizon of the Sacramento Valley. We've passed Mt. Shasta; the Cascades are behind us and the Sierras are too far away to be seen. I squint at the pink sunrise before snuggling back under the covers, reluctant to face the ordeal of a shampoo and wash-up in the tiny sink.

I want a shower. There is a common bath in the hall outside my room but the logistics are ugly: the door is too narrow for my chair, there's no bench or shower chair, and there is no direct or easy way to transfer into the stall.

The head porter lectured me yesterday about the danger of moveable chairs on trains and why Amtrak doesn't supply them. I think his excuse was bogus. Whoever designed the cars simply screwed up, or incorrectly assumed that people in chairs wouldn't want to bathe. The legal department may even have thrown a fit at the suggestion of placing an unanchored chair in the tiny cubicle. And the Union probably wasn't keen on their members becoming bath attendants. It's that kind of age we live in.

He offered the illogical alternative of an overturned milk crate which I could sit on. From the tone of his voice, I could tell he didn't expect me to accept. The suggestion brought visions of twisting or breaking a leg or cutting my rear, so I politely declined the offer. I'm one day into this journey and I don't want to lose it all because of a desire to take a shower.

It's the sink.

Naked, with a towel in my lap, I lather my scalp, rinse out the soap with tiny cupfuls of hot water, and utterly fail to keep the suds from running down my back. I roll away from the sink with every sway of the train. Frustrated, and with soap stinging my eyes, I finally hook my chin over the edge of the bowl and manage to stay in place. I wind up with a bruised chin but clean hair. With a wet washrag I clean under my armpits and get most of the soap that has gone down by back.

I dress and ring for Larry.

With the bedding removed, I sit, nibbling on a continental breakfast that is nowhere near as good as last night's steak dinner. The land outside is equally less appealing than was yesterday's Oregon countryside.

The Sacramento Valley is barren in comparison to Washington and Oregon. Mega-farms have gouged endless symmetrical furrows of toasted brown soil that stretch out of sight toward the horizon. Pickups speed down fronting roads and drag billowing dirt rooster tails as they ferry Hispanic workers and sacks of chemicals. Tractors are busy plowing up new furrows and move across the flat fields in tan dust clouds. Quonset huts with oiled yards have replaced the quaint barns and darling farmsteads of the Northwest.

We finally leave the valley and skirt San Francisco Bay. The choppy blue water, fishing boats, and scraggly bushes and trees are a paradise by comparison to what we've just left.

At noon we stop in Oakland. It's sunny and warm, leaves are still green, flowers are in bloom. The train stretches sleek against the long platform and is perfect for my first digital photograph, but we'll only stay a few minutes here so I'll have to hurry.

Larry, talking with a passenger who has already gotten out, gasps as he sees me pop a wheelie and move quickly toward the edge of the car's door. I drop twelve inches to the hard concrete, landing perfectly balanced on my back wheels. He smiles with relief. "Let me help you next time," he admonishes.

"Okay." *Like hell.*

At the front of the train, the engineer takes a picture of me leaning with one hand against the silvery locomotive. Afterwards, we huddle in the bright light, shielding the tiny screen to view the image. "Amazing!" he says. "You can see it right away!"

When we are back under way we soon leave the Bay area and enter the Salinas Valley. This was Steinbeck's setting for *Of Mice and Men*. The Gabilan Mountains rise low and rolling to the east, sun-baked brown with a scattering of dark trees. Small farms with weathered outbuildings checker the valley floor. Row crops, fruit trees, gardens; the stuff dust bowl immigrants' dreams were made of.

Steinbeck wrote about this land during the Great Depression. Yesterday, the Dow fell seven percent. The story dominated the front page of the *San Francisco Chronicle* slipped under my door this morning. I think about where I am and the happenstance of Steinbeck, the Depression, and the Dow's fall. Once in a while you stumble upon history in a way that hits home. I can easily picture Steinbeck out there amongst the vines and hayfields, observing the people of the 1930's, spending a day in laborer's boots, trying to record the essence of their suffering in a bleak and compelling work of fiction, hoping that it's significance won't be overlooked by future generations. It's surreal. The Dow's fall makes me think how easily it could all happen again. And how easily we forget to celebrate the wonderful gifts that come to us just by living in this country at this time in history.

We're in Los Angeles at midnight, two hours late. Passengers mill about, searching for baggage, meeting loved ones.

I've decided to hang out at LAX until the 8:30 AM flight to Honolulu. Checking into a hotel for six hours seems unnecessarily expensive. I slept well on the train and my excitement of starting the adventure has not yet subsided. I push aside the fear of being in the airport at night. What could happen?

I zoom down the ramp and through the tunnel, passing an electric cart packed with four elderly women and their bulky luggage. I imagine how they see me: bulging knapsack slung on the back of my chair and canvas suitcase crowding my lap, my head with its almost-bald spot moving like those wooden birds designed to peck at a glass of water: bob, peck, bob, peck, while my hands pump the rims.

The airport van driver turns out to be a writer for FOX television. We get into a good talk about writing. This temporary job of driving an airport van is a research project for him, as well as a little extra cash. He wants to learn what a driver's life is like. It's hard, he says, harder than he'd imagined.

Most drivers these days seem to be Indians, Africans, Lebanese and other foreigners scrambling for a foothold in America. They're usually in another dimension, possibly dreaming about their native homeland, maybe imagining how wonderful it will be to finally fit in here in America. But Ed is fully here, and fully frustrated with being here. His stint at carting people around ends in three days. I tell him I'll be on the road for maybe six months and he gives a low whistle.

Headed toward an uncertain evening, I relish Ed's company. He deposits me on the concrete ramp at the Delta Airlines sign. "Good luck!" he says, shaking my hand firmly. "Maybe we'll run into each other through our writing."

"I hope so. And good luck with your next three days."

The woman at Delta check-in says their lounge is closed, but she calls Alaska Airlines. Is their lounge open? No. I now begin to regret not getting a room. I'd hoped at least for a couch to lie down on. But I'm going to stick it out and not go off in search of a hotel room. It's just a few hours.

"You might want to go next door to the International Terminal," she offers. "I think some of the food vendors stay open all night."

I wheel out into the muggy night, breathing air thick with jet kerosene and car exhaust. Be tough, I tell myself. But I remember the old adage: *You get what you pay for.*

Inside the international terminal there are only a burger place and an ice cream shop still open. I buy a hamburger and fries and sit in a nearly empty sea of Formica-surfaced tables and chrome-and-fiberglass chairs.

With a growing sense of misadventure I settle down in this generic space I share with only a few maintenance workers and one young couple. I catch a few words of incomprehensible Spanish from the workers.

The couple consists of a gorgeous blonde with a massive glittering diamond ring and a handsome man in Bermudas, engrossed in a very private conversation. I think I recognize him from television. They finish their sodas, rise without seeming to notice anything or anyone around them, and purposefully walk away.

The maintenance crew disperses. Suddenly alone, I long for something to read. The magazine kiosk is closed. Occasionally, the kids in the burger joint and the ice cream shop glance in my direction. Do they think I'm homeless? Probably not, but I'm definitely not their usual evening customer.

It drags out into a long night. A *dumb* night, I keep telling myself. Why did I do this? I now crave the soft oblivion of a real bed. I imagine

Hawaii, a hot shower, and sleeping till noon.

At 3 AM the maintenance workers are patiently pushing dust mops, wet mops and buffers across the vast, empty floor below. The kids have vanished into their shops; there are no longer any customers to serve. Occasionally, one pokes a head out to check, then ducks back.

I lay my head on my arm but can't find a comfortable position. My elbow bruises against the Formica; my ear cauliflowers against my biceps; my back stiffens; my neck aches. I doze sporadically. When I open my eyes I have to squint and force tears to unstick my contact lenses.

At 5:30 AM a few people begin to wander through. I give up trying to sleep. The electronic reader board shows the first flight leaves at 7 AM. I buy a coffee, cool it with creamer and take several long sips, stretch my legs and twist my back until the vertebrae pop. The cobwebs clear and a little excitement returns.

I find a bathroom, rendered spotless by the maintenance crew. I splash cold water on my face, brush my teeth, and unsuccessfully try to wet down a cowlick of hair sticking up from the back of my head. Red lines spider-web the whites of my eyes. My head aches.

I hoist my pack onto the back of my chair, pull my suitcase off the countertop onto my lap, and roll off in search of the gate for the flight to Honolulu.

I've been a fool.

OCTOBER 29

Sick in Hawaii

ON THE FLIGHT TO HONOLULU I REALIZE I'VE PICKED UP A respiratory infection. The glands beneath my ears are tender. My sinuses run, my body aches.

Third day out on the road and I'm sick.

We land and I check into a hotel a stewardess recommends. It's expensive, but I'm too feverish to search for a cheap room and am just grateful to be somewhere comfortable. After a hot shower I collapse into bed.

By morning my chest tickles with congestion. Coughing fails to dislodge the phlegm. I'm exhausted despite sixteen hours of sleep. The words *viral pneumonia* keep coming to mind but I push that thought away, hoping this is a simple cold.

The irony is that my pre-trip planning has included inoculations for Hepatitis A and B, Yellow Fever, Typhus, Encephalitis and Tetanus-Diphtheria. My TB skin test was negative. I reviewed my immunological history (bacterial pneumonia vaccination; mumps, measles and chicken pox as a child) with the public health nurse. But the common cold? You can't plan for everything.

I skip breakfast. A shower fails to relieve the chills which now rack my body. I drink several glasses of water and crawl back into bed. I'm regularly hacking up gobs of brown crud. It's impossible to sleep. I turn on the TV and try not to become too depressed.

By noon, I'm starved. I dress a body that feels like one large bruise. In the hotel coffee shop I order a tuna salad sandwich and two glasses of orange juice. The food stays down. "Tomorrow, I'll be better," I mumble over and over, like a mantra.

The next morning I'm worse. Phlegm rattles in my chest. I wheeze when I breathe. My fever has risen to 101 degrees. Should I catch a plane home? I could get well and then start over. But that's bogus. I resolve to *make* myself well.

I begin to drink everything I can lay my hands on: tea, juice, soda and countless glasses of water; more than a gallon by the end of the day. I pee like the proverbial fire hydrant. The phlegm now comes up easily; the brown lumps have vanished. By the time I fall into bed at 7 PM my fever has broken. I'm beat, but on the mend.

My biggest fear has been that it wasn't a cold, but a bladder infection. With no feeling below my rib cage I feel no pain to warn of an infection. Instead, I must watch for more subtle clues such as small and frequent voids, cold legs, and cloudy or smelly urine. Ultimately, it's only a lab test that can confirm a urinary tract problem.

I've brought antibiotics, prescribed by my doctor for just such an emergency, but I'm reluctant to use them. I'm also not keen on trying to find a doctor who understands a paraplegic's particular needs. My worst bladder infection ever came from a routine catheterization by an inept urologist. It was days before I figured it out on my own; the urologist never owned up to causing the problem.

Colds get better quickly. Bladder infections can linger for weeks or months, and if they get into your kidneys the damage can be permanent. Throughout the day I've touched my legs and they've remained warm. My voids are large. My urine is clear. These are hopeful signs but are no certainty. Only when I'm well will I know it was just a passing illness.

I fight off a lingering depression that threatens to disintegrate my adventure into a nightmare. I remind myself to take this one day at a time and to hope for the best.

November 1

Recovery in Honolulu

On the third day in Honolulu my energy returns and I finally feel well enough to call the Harbor Master and ask about ships between Hawaii and Australia. If they tell me to get down to the docks, I can now justify the risk of boarding a ship. But my enthusiasm and optimism about finding an ocean passage are short-lived.

"There's nothing like what you want," the man says. "The only regular ships between here and Australia are cement ships. They don't take passengers."

I hang up, wondering if this is true; I'm used to getting the runaround from administrative types when they learn I'm in a wheelchair.

I call Hawaii's largest freight shipping line. "We don't take passengers," I'm told. "It's too much of a hassle. We just handle freight, mostly cement."

"Do you know anyone who does take passengers?"

"No. I don't think anyone does. The liability insurance costs too much. There's no profit in it for us."

I call other companies. None carry passengers from Hawaii to Australia. I feel foolish.

I languish in my hotel for two more days, watching television until I'm sick of CNN updates. I watch *The Rocky Horror Picture Show* three times on the movie channel.

By now my frustration is pushing me to do something, anything, even if it turns out to be wrong. Somehow I've got to regain my enthusiasm. It's been only one short week, and I've spent most of it in a room that's begun to feel like a prison.

Four unplanned weeks stretch ahead. It's not until December that I've booked Australia and New Zealand for rooms, trains, and my dive on the Barrier Reef. Moving those events up is impossible, especially the week of sponsored lodging the Holiday Inn in Cairns is providing.

I ponder finding a cheap hotel in Honolulu and sitting the time out, but where's the adventure in that? I decide it's time to get off my butt and do something.

I considering going to either Fiji or American Samoa. But a tropical climate seems a poor place to recover from a cold. A quick check on the Internet tells me it's in the seventies in Sydney. Perfect. I email a Sydney B&B with an accessible room; it's available as soon as I want to arrive.

The earliest available economy fare that a local travel agent finds for me is a red-eye in five days, with a four-hour layover in Fiji. If I'm lucky I'll find a place at the airport to put my feet up; they often swell up on long flights, and the only way to counteract this is to elevate them, something that is impossible in economy class unless there's a row of empty seats to lie down on. This flight is fully booked so I'll be sitting for six hours.

In the end I decide this is my best alternative. I buy the ticket.

No longer trapped by illness, and looking forward to the next step in my young journey, I begin to relax and enjoy Honolulu, gradually rebuilding my endurance. At a nearby mall I drink fruit smoothies, eat pasta and sushi, and am amused by the elegant strut of skinny Japanese girls wearing Spice Girls pumps and carrying Gucci bags.

There is so much diversity here, unlike my rural hometown. The

Chinese chain smoke on their lunch breaks; almost no one back home smokes in public. The sidewalks flow with young people tanned and healthy from beach life, contrasted with the occasional pasty-skinned European wearing heavy clothing as if the sun were poison; back home people are in winter coats. My wheelchair seems to fit comfortably into this human menagerie; no one gives me a second look; in almost any small town back home I get first and second looks, but only when they think I'm not watching.

I haven't gone out at night, but two days before I leave I can't resist. The half-moon hangs low and bright, framed by glimmering stars. The air is thick with the perfume of jasmine and frangipani. A salty breeze stirs the palms. Friday night has the city packed with people. Cars jam the intersections.

Loud music fills the crowded *Hard Rock Café* as I pass through the double doors. Many of the diners are Japanese. Not *American* Japanese, but *Japanese* Japanese in tourist clothing: Nikes, vivid floral shirts, white cotton slacks, sandals. Some wear flower leis. They have come here to experience Americana; to be able to say: "Been there, done that." This is what the people of the affluent Western world seem to have come to. The people of the last quarter of the twentieth century should be called the *Been There, Done That Generations*.

I devour chicken and fries, washed down with a yeasty micro-brew. Not healthy, but it tastes great. And I decide I've earned this finger lickin' decadence.

Tipsy from the beer, I return to my room on the seventh floor. Lying in the dark, I listen to the nearby elevators slide up and down, and unexpectedly, my fear of running short of funds surfaces. I must somehow cut expenses to make up for this pricey room. I'll have to ask people to help me find bargains or give me discounts. And that will come hard.

After my skiing accident, I was determined not to become dependent so I refused all help that wasn't absolutely essential. I wanted to
prove I could do everything by myself. Now I can't afford the whim of
isolation. I must break this long-entrenched pattern of behavior. I know
it won't come easy.

November 10

Agents and Indians

AFTER ELEVEN DAYS IN HONOLULU I SAY GOODBYE TO THE HOTEL reception staff and the waitresses and barmen, all of whom have become friends. I tell the doorman I need a cab but he insists all guests are taken to the airport in a limo. He assures me it costs the same. It ends up costing ten bucks more.

I've never been in a limousine. I sit in the wide seat, feeling like a celebrity, feeling safe as we shoot through nearly deserted back streets. Then I remember Princess Diana and her fatal Paris accident. I pull the seat belt and shoulder harness across my body.

When I bought the air ticket for Sydney I was told my visa for Australia was automatically included. I now learn the agent screwed up when he made the booking.

"You need a Visa number," the woman at check-in says suspiciously. "Did they give you another slip of paper when you got your ticket?"

"No." This, I think, is what I get for buying a discount ticket from a two-person booth on the street in downtown Honolulu.

She gives me a tired smile. "Don't worry. I can get you one electronically." She turns to her computer. I'm suddenly glad to have come early.

During my twenty-five years in a wheelchair I've been treated considerately by most people who work in the travel industry. But occasionally I encounter someone whose life seems to consist of one long bad-hair day.

A person obsessed with crossing t's and dotting i's.

The helpful agent is still busy on her computer when another agent, in her fifties, comes from behind a far counter, zeroing in on me like a grade school teacher on recess patrol. Working up a frown as she approaches, her hair perm'd like Doris Day in a 1950's movie, she strides purposefully as her polished shoes click on the tile, wearing a starched uniform that is lintless and pinfold crisp. She stands before me.

"Are you going to Fiji?" she asks gently but firmly.

The agent at the computer ignores her.

"Yes." I wonder how she knows, then remember from the reader board that it's the only flight this airline has listed for the next several hours.

"It's six hours to Fiji."

"Uh huh."

"So … do you take a pill, or something?"

I'm a little stunned. Is she talking about taking a pee on a long flight? A pill? Is there such a thing? I imagine a commercial for such a product. A man stands in a neat blue suit, holding a small case filled with vials of colored pills. With a game show announcer's sonorous voice he says: "Take the blue pill if you don't want to pee for three hours. Take the orange pill for six. Take the red pill and you'll be dry all day long!"

I try not to laugh or to look amused. She's serious. And idiots hate to be laughed at.

I'm tempted to remind her that all long-range jets have collapsible aisle chairs and that the attendants are trained to assist wheelchair passengers to the bathroom. It's a requirement of the *Americans with Disabilities Act*. It's called *reasonable accommodation*. I'm not feeling particularly charitable so I give a half-smile and wait quietly, hoping she'll go find someone else to pester. No such luck.

"Well, the bathroom," she continues. "How do you handle it if you have to use the bathroom?"

Does she have the power to keep me from getting on the plane? The woman helping me with the electronic visa quietly continues to work on her computer, so I dismiss this fear. I hold my silence.

The nosy agent is not satisfied, but there is a tiny crack of uncertainty in her voice. She tries to justify herself.

"I knew a crew who wouldn't let a man on because he couldn't get to the bathroom."

"Oh," I say nonchalantly, wishing I'd said, "I take a green pill," when she first asked. But it's too late.

"Well, I handle it okay," I add dismissively, as if she were dense for not knowing.

"Oh." She is perplexed by my answer. Then a look comes across her face as if she suddenly understands. She's faking. She doesn't really want to know. She turns, walks back the way she came, disappears though a door.

I'm tough enough to not let this woman disturb me. But someone new to a chair might be more easily intimidated. This type of ignorant bullying is needless and hurtful.

The printer finally grinds out my visa. I get a boarding pass.

I now crave a good book to read to pass the time but the newsstand stocks only formula potboilers. *Esquire's* fiction for November isn't interesting. I opt for TV in the bar.

It's 9 PM, and a lot of tired bodies are slumped in metal chairs next to bulky suitcases and boxes of pineapples. Their flower leis are already beginning to wilt inside plastic sacks on the tables. They're headed back to jobs, to winter, and their flights won't get them home before morning. Their few days in paradise have fled by.

I share a table with a forty-something couple. *The X Files*, which I never watch, is on. The woman volunteers facts about the characters and the plot but the story line eludes me.

"You have to watch it every week," she says, "to understand what's happening." But it must not be that interesting because she soon gives up on the TV and talks to me. We talk about their home in Virginia. She asks where I'm from.

"Washington State."

"Then you must be headed home through San Francisco?" the husband asks.

"No, I'm going on to Sydney."

Blank look.

"Australia."

"Oh, well … have a good flight," he says sheepishly. They get up to leave. I've inadvertently acted like a snob and I'm embarrassed.

Time drags. I find a cafeteria, eat a sandwich and a bowl of soup, and then find my gate. I slouch in my chair with half-closed eyes until the agent comes over.

"Sir?"

"Yes."

"We'll board you first."

The plane takes off just after midnight. It's half-empty, and I wonder why the man who sold me the ticket said it was full.

Being disabled and getting on first can be a great advantage. I'm able to lay claim to an entire row of unassigned seats. After dinner, I have the luxury of stretching out full length. Nearby, a baby cries and an old man coughs in the dry cabin air. I put in my earplugs and quickly fall asleep.

The attendant wakes me after what seems like a nap, but hours have passed. "We're one hundred and fifty miles from Fiji," she says. "Time to get up."

She returns with a hot washcloth. I rub bits of tear crust from the corners of my eyes, gingerly put in my contacts, then twist and stretch to work out the kinks.

We de-plane at 4:30 AM. Those in transit are allowed to bypass customs. Since there are stairs on the usual route, two men in military uniforms take me through a locked side-door, down a motorized luggage lift, and back out into the waiting area. From the hundreds of seats I choose a place near the bathrooms. The officers lay my backpack and suitcase on the end of a row of chairs and leave.

Shops selling liquor, perfume, T-shirts, mugs, woodcarvings and other junk border the seating area. I'm disinclined to search for a souvenir. Already my luggage seems too heavy. When I packed, everything seemed necessary. Now I'm unsure. Do I really need an extra inner tube, or is the patch kit sufficient? Do I need three extra pairs of pants? I'd like to dump the language books and tapes and the mini-cassette player, though I'm reluctant to give up on learning at least a few phrases of French, Italian and Spanish. I now regret every foreign language elective I skipped in high school and college.

I'm sitting near an Indian man who was on my earlier flight. He's handsome, darkly complected, distinguished, in his mid-fifties. We strike up a conversation. I learn he was born in Fiji but has lived in Canada for three decades. He's headed to Brisbane.

I ask him about Fiji. It sounds like a nice place. Better than I had imagined, though I'm uncertain why so many military police are circulating among the passengers. He tells me that since the coup in 1976 Fiji is more democratic. The number of police is more about employment than security.

"The economy is good now. The dollar is strong."

"What are the largest industries?

"Gold."

"Gold?" That seems illogical. Fiji is tiny. The two sizeable islands are less than 300 square miles each, and many of the other 100 islands are too small to inhabit. It's difficult to picture gold mines.

"Oh yes, there is much gold here. And sugar cane, tuna fishing, tourists." Those latter industries make more sense to me. *Never judge a book by its cover*, I remind myself.

I've been drinking pop and hot tea since getting off the plane. While we talk, my leg bag fills. I need to empty it. The bathroom has a narrow spring-closing door that I'd never squeeze through with luggage.

"I need to use the bathroom," I finally confess. "Would you mind watching my bags for just a minute?"

"Of course I can."

I'm nervous about leaving everything important in the custody of a stranger, so I hurry. When I come out he's still there, patiently watching a long line of Japanese schoolgirls boarding a 747.

"Would you watch mine?" he asks politely. "I want to look in the duty free."

"Certainly." I sit, feeling pleased by his trust, but just a bit embarrassed at having harbored doubts about him.

He is gone for some time. When he returns he carries a sack containing two bottles of liquor, one the local rum, which he says is excellent. It sells for a ridiculously low price, but the last thing I need is more weight. I'm not even sure what rum tastes like.

For the next three hours we take turns watching each other's luggage. Some people I would never trust like this. Before leaving home I read a book: *The Gift of Fear*. It said to believe your gut feelings; they're seldom wrong. Our ancestors survived on their instincts. People in the modern world have forgotten to listen to the inner voice of their instinct. People get into trouble when they ignore the niggling doubt, the little chill. Intuition can be as reliable as a compass, but you must choose to recognize and follow it. I sense that I could trust this Indian with my life if it became necessary.

Indians have always impressed me, though I've met very few and have never known one well. I remember an Indian family that lived down the street from me in Redmond. When the patriarch came from India to visit he used to take long evening walks. A distinguished man with white hair, he moved slowly, his back ramrod straight, hands perpetually clasped behind his back. He held his head high, eyes scanning constantly as if to savor every tree, bird and flower. He was educated and cultured. I said "Hello" twice from my yard but never received more than a polite nod in return, though from his daughter I knew he spoke English well.

My Indian's flight is called, we wish each other well, and as he walks off I immediately miss his company.

Finally, the Sydney boarding announcement blares on the speakers.

By coincidence, I'm seated next to an Indian woman on the flight. She says she has converted to Christianity but refrains from asking about my beliefs. She talks about her daughter and the grandchildren she is traveling to visit and tells me she was born and grew up in Fiji.

I tell her about my travel project.

"You should have spent some time in Fiji," she mildly scolds. "You would like it."

"I didn't know anything about Fiji."

"There are many beautiful islands. And nice beaches."

"I'm not much of a beach person."

"You would like the people."

"I'm sure I would."

"You will have to come back to Fiji someday and write about it."

When our meals come she closes her eyes. Her lips move in silent prayer for two minutes, then she opens her eyes and looks at me. "I have much to be thankful for," she says and, without further explanation, begins to eat.

I think about this declaration. About her. About our conversation. Not once has she questioned my travel capabilities. She hasn't drawn comparisons to anyone else in a wheelchair. She is a woman, Indian, a Fiji citizen, a devout Christian dressed in a colorful red, orange and yellow sarong and wearing much gold jewelry. We couldn't be more different. Yet neither of us has tried to convince the other we are better. We've simply shared our time together.

She has reminded me how easy it can be to be at peace with myself.

November 12

Grandma Mable

PAUL URE MEETS ME AT THE AIRPORT. HE AND HIS WIFE SYL own a homestay in the posh Sydney suburb of Rose Bay. I'm exhausted from traveling for twenty-four hours so I spend the afternoon unpacking, visiting with Paul and Syl, and trying to unwind. The day is cloudy but warm; the scents of jacaranda and star jasmine drift through the open windows; a gentle rain begins to fall in the early evening. By seven I'm ready for bed and I quickly fall into a deep sleep.

I dream of my grandmother Mable. She and I talk about our feelings for each other. I'm preparing to leave on this trip. I anguish about delaying my departure, feeling I must leave, but somehow know she won't be alive when I return. She tells me it's okay to go.

Mable was my father's mother and the only grandparent I knew. After my parents divorced in 1966, she and Mom remained close. Dad resisted paying child support and this must have hurt Mable. He also moved away, making it difficult to arrange father-son activities. It was tough having a dad in name only. During the sixties, divorce was still a disgrace, not just for the couple but also for the children. Grandma became a surrogate for our lost father.

Times were tough for Mom, who never remarried. She was raising two boys. She first worked as a cook, then in real estate, eventually landing a state job which for the first time provided a decent and consistent

34

income and health benefits.

During the early struggle to keep afloat financially it was Mable who helped when Mom came up short on the house payment or needed a replacement car for a beater that had finally died. When Mom needed someone to watch us we went to Grandma's. Ken and I always looked forward to peanut butter and strawberry jam sandwiches, a tall glass of cold milk, and candy bars that were stashed at the back of a certain kitchen drawer. There was a cherry tree to climb out in her huge yard, and a fifty-foot hedge from which we could cut whip-swords or spears. My late grandfather's shop held a treasury of odds and ends he'd saved since the Depression. We were never bored; we were always loved. I still remember the twinkle in grandma's eyes when Ken and I zoomed into the yard on our bikes and scrambled into her kitchen with ravenous looks and the hope that she had baked an apple pie that morning.

Mable's energy was amazing. Even in her eighties, and missing the sight in one eye, she continued to drive. She had a cabin in the Methow Valley, ninety miles north of Chelan. Summertimes, she'd load my brother and me into her blue Lark station wagon and we'd head up-country for a week. She said this was to give Mom a break but I'm certain it was more an excuse to spend time with us. In a very real way, we were a replacement for our father whom she was gradually losing to alcohol and emphysema.

After the long drive, during which she rarely went faster than forty-five on the twisting two-lane road, she would lie down on her bed at the cabin with a cold washrag on her forehead. "You boys just go off and play for a while," she'd caution.

We'd grab our fly rods and fish for trout in the river, or corner snakes and frogs in the rocks along the creek that cut through her five acres, or stalk off into the woods to hunt birds and chipmunks with bb guns.

If it was a really hot day, and in that high mountain country the mid-afternoon temperature could easily reach triple digits, we'd retreat into the huge metal culvert the creek ran through under the highway, where we had built a platform from boards scavenged from a nearby disintegrating barn. The creek chilled the corrugated steel and we'd hang our feet in the icy water. Once we had cooled down we would go out and work on the rock dam we were constructing at the culvert mouth, backing water into a pool nearly deep enough to swim in.

By the time we returned to grandma's cabin there would be a skillet of fried chicken and a bowl of potato salad set out on a red-and-white checked tablecloth. We would gorge ourselves, then go to bed with the sound of wind in the pines, toads ratcheting down by the river and crickets chorusing from the forest.

She died in February 1972, while I was in the hospital with my broken back. Mom later told me Grandma was intent upon coming to Seattle to help in my rehabilitation. She died in her sleep. There was nothing I could do about it and until this dream I have regretted not being there.

I'm not a believer in the mystical or supernatural. But I'm convinced the human soul can heal itself in remarkable and unexplainable ways. I was struggling today, wondering how I would fill three unplanned weeks in Sydney. My subconscious has responded with the gift of this dream. Adventure is never more than a heartbeat away if you have your eyes open and your imagination running up to speed. In grandma's house, adventure was easily found in an upstairs storage space, out in grandpa's shop, or in a hard fought card game of canasta. I'm reminded by my dream to relax and take things as they come. It's a good sign.

NOVEMBER 13

Improvised Accessibility

THE NEXT DAY I UNPACK MY LAPTOP COMPUTER AND TRY TO LOG onto the Internet using the Ure's phone line. With my international server it's supposed to be simple. It's not.

What I do now is akin to what most guys do when lost in a car. Instead of asking for directions, they stubbornly try to find their own way. I don't call the help number. Instead, I blunder through the command screens of *Windows 95* and *Netscape*.

After hours of frustration, I find the cure. The help program directs me to type in a seemingly meaningless code: *X3*. Presto! I log on and can finally send articles and photos to the newspaper, research future destinations, and get in touch with my house-sitter.

But I'm still three weeks ahead of schedule.

There are worse places to be. In the Pacific Northwest, snow is falling. Here, the jacaranda trees are flames of lavender at the height of their bloom; spring is bursting a green canopy over the suburbs; the air is a perfume of star and orange jasmine and wisteria. Cicadas and frogs fill the warm night air with song. And a family of kookaburas, cackling with mad laughter, roosts in the Norfolk Pine by the deck.

I finish my second column for the *Wenatchee World* newspaper, glumly titled: *Ill in Oahu*. To counter this pessimism I start writing a piece about how lovely Sydney is this time of year.

37

By default, a small adventure comes my way. Syl needs my room for two nights for a previous booking she can't cancel. I decide to take the ferry out to Manly and find a hotel.

The moderately priced hotels all say "No" to the wheelchair when I call. I'm eventually referred to an expensive hotel with an international name. I knew I'd occasionally get stuck, but the rate is a shock. I decide to take it. It's only for two days.

Lodging is always a challenge for someone in a wheelchair. Newer hotels usually accept wheelchairs, but they're costly. Older hotels rarely have elevators, level entries, wide doorways or spacious bathrooms. Homestays, B&B's and backpacker accommodations are often the worst for accessibility because most of them have steps and dinky bathrooms. For what I want to accomplish persistence is necessary. Because if I stayed only at places that advertise themselves as accessible, this trip would cost double what I have in my budget.

When I'm on the road and can't find a room that is truly wheelchair accessible, I can still usually figure out a way to make a place work, at least for a night or two. If there is no shower bench I can usually scrounge up a plastic deck chair. I've sat on folded towels in a tub when a chair isn't to be found. If the bathroom doorway is too narrow for my wheelchair to pass through, I can transfer onto an ordinary chair and slide myself around. Of course, if the room door is too narrow, or if all rooms require climbing steps, I am forced to pass and look for other accommodations.

"How do you manage?" people frequently ask. I reply, "You have to be flexible and have a sense of humor." I usually add, "I've never had to sleep under a bridge!" Figuratively and literally, that's the truth. But if had to sleep under a bridge, I'd figure out a way to make it work. You adjust to the place, rather than demand that it adjust to you. And when you go in with this kind of an attitude, it's surprising how helpful the owners can suddenly become.

NOVEMBER 18

Manley

ON THE MORNING FERRY TO MANLY, THE *SYDNEY MORNING HERALD's* headline reports that Muslim terrorists have killed seventy tourists in Egypt's Valley of the Queens. They easily penetrated the security cordon around what has been advertised as Egypt's safest tourist attraction. Japanese, Swedes and others were shot by gunmen who then fled. Egyptian soldiers later caught up with and killed them, but no one expects their slaughter to lessen the danger to western visitors. The U.S. and Australian state departments are cautioning travelers not to go to Egypt until the issue is clarified by Egyptian security forces.

I had hoped to go to Egypt. The Nile seemed so intriguing. But the wheelchair makes me the easiest of targets, and being an American puts me at the top of their list. I'm a realist. I could be taken hostage by the maid in my hotel, never mind men with Uzis and rocket-propelled grenades.

I decide to strike Egypt from my list of possible places to visit, and turn my attention to the boat I'm on.

Sydney ferries come in several shapes and sizes. The sleek jet catamarans (*Jetcats* and *Rivercats*). The old double-deckers which resemble children's bathtub toys, still in service after half a century. And the larger boats able to handle the open ocean. I'm on the last type, a ship called the *Lady Northcott*, which is capable of carrying hundreds of passengers.

These grand old dames of the sea were built in England and piloted out shortly after WWII. She cuts a deep wake as she ploughs steadily through the swell coming in through the harbor mouth from the Pacific.

As the bluffs to the north slowly slide past, a man in his seventies walks by grasping the hand of a two-year-old boy who would much rather run than walk with Grandpa. I smile at the child. He smiles back. The man pauses.

"It's nice to see you can still smile at the kids."

"Yes."

"Do you know what I mean?"

"Yeah."

I know exactly what he means. He's talking about the loss of innocence in our modern world. In this man's youth, you could trust a stranger, both in Australia and in America. Smiling at a child didn't brand you a potential pervert. Where and when have we lost that?

I have a theory.

The media focus upon the worst pedophile, spouse-beater or rapist. *Experts* then describe how *these kinds of people* are everywhere, even in places least expected. Deviancy becomes the standard. We focus upon evil and forget that good exists. People live in fear. We forget the dignity of a smile. We look for the worst, and turn toward isolation as if it were the only available form of self-defense. Aggression becomes the way to resolve disputes. We are losing our capacity to express love, or even to understand it. Everyone hates this shift toward darkness, but no one seems to know how to counteract it.

One nice thing about being in a wheelchair is that you aren't threatening. I have the privilege of smiling at children. I treasure it.

They come around again and both grandfather and grandson beam at me.

"Have a good visit," he says.

"Thanks."

MANLY STRADDLES THE NORTHERN SPIT OF THE SYDNEY HARBOR entrance. It has one of the nicest beaches on the Pacific, a lazy crescent that catches two miles of open ocean and breaks it into gentle waves. It also boasts attractions like *OCEANWORLD*, whose huge sign proclaims: *Shark Feeding 11:15 AM, 2 PM, 4 PM*. I don't bother. I plan see the real thing when I dive on the Barrier Reef. Watching sharks tear into a bloody chunk of carcass meat in a big tank isn't my idea of fun. Just the thought of it gives me the creeps.

On my first morning, I'm sipping *flat white* (coffee with milk), eating apple strudel, and people watching from a French patesserie. The sky is flawless. A breeze whispers in from the Pacific. This is an idyllic in paradise.

You can dine in Manly in restaurants that feature Italian, Indonesian, Malay, Thai, German, Mexican, Spanish, Moroccan, Japanese, Chinese and nouveau Australian (kangaroo, barramundi, ostrich and crocodile) food. The eateries are often side-by-side. It's a shame the countries of the world can't coexist as peacefully as do the restaurants of Manly.

Sydneysiders come here to escape the bustle of urban life. Most of the faces are young, vibrant and happy. They are mostly an athletic crowd who preen to be seen. Hard bodies.

I pay my bill and go cruising down the boardwalk. Suddenly, I rediscover a rough corner of my soul. I feel eyes upon my wheelchair. So many people are here for the beach, a place off-limits to me because the wheelchair and sand are incompatible. I'm decidedly the odd man out. I haven't felt this way in years.

When I left the hospital in April of 1972, I went through many months of feeling the way I do now. I'd be rolling down the street and suddenly wonder if people were watching *that guy in the wheelchair*. I was already self-conscious as a seventeen-year-old. With a wheelchair added to the picture, insecurity became a monster.

It took a lot of work to rebuild my identity. I threw myself into confronting my fears by joining an encounter group. I read books on self-image. I resumed dating. I chose psychology for my undergraduate major. Gradually, I became comfortable with who I was. A new *me* evolved. I saw myself as sensitive. I regained strength in my upper body. There was nothing I could do about thinning legs, but with frequent stretching to maintain range of motion I at least had flexibility, if not muscle mass. I directed my energies toward college and gaining admission to law school.

If someone saw me as crippled, that was his or her problem. My philosophy became: Don't look at the ten percent I can't do, look at the ninety percent I *can* do.

I managed to get through those early years and continued to redefine myself as I entered the practice of law.

I became more and more comfortable because I surrounded myself with things I understood and could control. In my practice, I was the boss. People came to me, bared their souls, and paid for my advice. I owned a nice home in an upscale neighborhood. People knew me in the places where I hung out. In a word, I was *safe*.

In Manly, no one knows what I'm capable of. And in a dark corner of my mind, I am surprised to discover a little voice saying: *They see you as a cripple*.

I didn't come to Manly expecting to search my soul. I don't like it. But I must deal with it.

I get through the day. But by evening, I'm back to analyzing. I realize that I'm angry about three things that seem unfair: It's difficult to find social situations where I can interact. My wheelchair makes it awkward for people to include me in activities. And people don't know what I'm capable of, and they seem scared to ask.

Sitting in my room, staring at the wall, I realize that I'm the one with the problem. I hold the power to change things. I recall the man and his wife I met that very first morning, on the platform, waiting to board the *Coast Starlight* in Seattle. I now see that I dealt with that situation poorly. I had a chance to help him better understand what it's like to be in a wheelchair, and I blew it. I was insensitive. He, at least, was trying.

I knew this trip, and breaking away from friends, home, and routines would change me. I had no idea that it might not be fun. This lesson hurts a lot more than I would like.

November 21

Outsiders

If I felt like an outsider in Manly, on my return to Sydney I see someone who reminds me what it truly means to be outside.

Looking like a cross between Albert Einstein and Salvadore Dali, he sits on a green bench in back of *Circular Quay*. Drooping white handlebar moustache; cotton candy fly-away hair; red shirt and baggy brown pants probably last washed by rain. Thick horn-rims perched on a substantial nose, his gaze is fixed upon the open newspaper he holds stiff and high, as if it contained tomorrow's racing results.

I guess him to be well educated, but the half-filled, black plastic scavenger's bag at his feet reveals how far he has fallen.

It's a perfect summer day: 80° with a light breeze and spotty clouds that earlier tried to rain. This stranger I now watch shares this day with me, but I feel more in control of my life. He continues to read, oblivious to my glances. After five minutes, when I walk through the breezeway to the docks, he has moved only to turn a page.

At Wharf Five a few weary men and women in dark suits await the 7:05 Rose Bay ferry. Most of the lawyers, bankers, accountants and office workers have already fled to the suburbs or to a pub on this Friday evening. In the weary eyes of these last to leave, I see the contemplation of a cold drink while their bare feet frame the TV screen or a vista from a deck.

There are also a few tourists at the dock. A man with a beer gut wears a souvenir shirt and a straw hat. His dowdy wife clutches a shopping bag and a black leather purse hangs by a long strap from her shoulder. Near the boarding ramp a young couple shouldering packframes stand close. Japanese parents with two young children scan a ferry schedule with wide, uncertain eyes.

A mother resignedly watches her daughter of six whoop with joy as the *Dawn Fraser* jetcat approaches and revs its motors into reverse, flooding the air with sweet diesel and creaking the wharf's pilings with backwash. The mate casually loops a thick sisal rope around a post and snugs the catamaran to a stop. We who wait troop over the humped aluminum ramp and settle into comfortably upholstered seats.

As we glide toward Rose Bay, I ponder how many dispossessed people there are in the world. Not just the homeless man near the Quay, but also people like the South African I'll call *John* whom I've met at the homestay.

He's in his mid-forties, owns a thriving business in Johannesburg, is a father and husband. And he hopes to expatriate his family from South Africa to Australia in the near future.

"We had two house servants," John says, explaining why it's unusual for him to be doing a load of laundry. "I've only just bought myself one of those steamers, for getting the wrinkles out of clothes." He smiles about the accomplishment and I see the enormity of the adjustment he is going through. I've done my own laundry for years.

John has been house shopping, unsuccessfully. The waterfront property he wants is far too expensive for his devalued South African rand, even though he is considered wealthy back home.

"Of course, things had to change," he says. "It wasn't right, the way the blacks were treated after the Afrikaners took over in nineteen forty-eight and began to enforce apartheid.

"But it's hard for us. The exchange on our rand is so low it's impossible to replace our style of life. We're starting over here. But there are things more important than material possessions. Things like safety. Our children are full of fear in South Africa. People get pulled from their cars and shot. And if you're a white man over forty and you lose your job, you can't hope to get another one because of the black preference.

"There used to be two South Africas. The white one was 'first world' and the black one was 'third world.' But now there's only one, and it's all shifting towards third world. The medical care isn't what it used to be. There are black men without training running companies who don't do as good a job as a white man." He looks wistful for a moment.

"But it had to happen. Because the way the blacks were treated ... it just wasn't right."

As I listen, I hear the same kind of desperation that my law clients suffer. Women going through divorces. Partners going through break-ups. Car crash survivors trying to recover their health while being denied medical benefits by the other driver's insurance company.

I remember the fellow on the bench reading the paper. What expectations did he have as a young man? What changed his life so dramatically?

I had a friend, now dead, who once was a physicist. During the second half of his life he washed dishes and sold sundries at a convenience store. He died in a single-room apartment, alone. I never asked Don what caused him to run away.

The downhill slide begins when you let the random events of life derail your plans. Discouraged, you become detached and no longer find the energy to care. The magic of believing disappears.

As I watch John fold his clothes, I realize that we all have burdens.

And that the key to overcoming them is remaining intrigued by the wonder of life itself.

Sydney University

THE WEATHER HEATS UP AFTER I MOVE FROM THE SWANK SUBURB of Rose Bay to International House, a dorm at Sydney University. I'll spend a week here before flying to Cairns and a first experience with scuba gear. Daytime temperatures climb into the nineties. *El Ninô* has brought a hot summer to this part of the world. Bush fires are burning throughout New South Wales. The air is thick with smoke except when the wind blows in from the ocean.

There are escapes from the heat. The student center is air-conditioned. And the Olympic-sized pool is close. I start to swim half a mile every other day, regaining much of the strength I lost during my Honolulu illness.

There are benefits to staying at International House that outweigh the simplicity of the room and the heat that radiates through the brick during the afternoons. It is a huge bargain in an expensive city, costing just $25 per day, which includes three meals. There's also a special wheelchair bathroom with a shower bench and an accessible toilet and sink.

And there are the students: a racial and cultural mix different from what I've experienced in U.S. colleges and universities. I meet kids from Malaysia, Indonesia, Singapore, Taiwan, India, Sri Lanka, Thailand, France, Great Britain, the Netherlands and Germany. There are Moslems, Hindus and Buddhists, from cultures as diverse as Tamal, Nepalese,

Turkish, Arab, Indian and Thai.

It takes courage to join the students for my first cafeteria meal. My social skills with young strangers are rusty. And I find myself suddenly sensitive about being in a wheelchair. On my first evening, I nervously pull into the only empty spot at a large round table.

"Are you here for a conference?" a twenty-something Taiwanese woman asks as I put my tray down.

"No, I'm traveling."

"How did you come to International House?"

"I was looking for an affordable place to stay. Someone suggested here. Besides, I like being around students better than being stuck with tourists in a hotel." Many smile in agreement at this observation and I feel a bit more comfortable.

They keep asking questions, and I finally start to talk about the book. I'm surprised by their interest.

A student from Hong Kong encourages me to add her city to my itinerary. "You would like it!" she says enthusiastically. "There is so much to do."

"It's out of my way. I was just thinking of somewhere on the Malaysian Peninsula, then Bangkok."

"But airfare is so cheap right now," she insists, looking disappointed. "You could fly from Singapore. It's only four hours."

The recent devaluation of Asian currencies makes travel in Asia a bargain. I could try to fit it within my budget. I tell her I'll think about it.

What I want to say is that not speaking Chinese makes travel to Hong Kong a bit daunting. I keep hoping she'll suggest a friend or family member to show me around but she never does. One thing you learn about being in a wheelchair is that many people are quick to suggest something, but few are willing to put themselves on the line to help you make it happen. Dating is much that way. I have plenty of married woman friends who encourage me to keep looking for "the right woman." They insist there is someone for me and all I have to do is keep the faith. But when I talk to single women the subject almost never comes up, and I've yet to have someone set me up on a blind date with one of their friends or family members. The dual standard is real. But I digress … .

The next day I meet Eric from the Netherlands. He says he'll be home when I reach Europe. He gives me his email address, assuring me he'll read the Internet articles and follow the progress of my trip. He asks if I like painters and says there is an art museum near where he lives that is dedicated to Van Gough.

"I love Van Gough."

"Then you should come and see the museum."

Living at International House also opens a new perspective on America. These are some of the brightest foreign students, including several doctoral candidates. Some have visited or studied in America. And their impression of America is that it is a violent, dangerous place.

At first I'm defensive. I tell my new friends that I've never seen anyone shot and I've never seen a gun fired in anger. On visits to supposedly dangerous places like New Orleans and Washington, D.C. I've felt safe. I tell them this over and over.

No one is convinced.

"It's our news media. They focus on a few dangerous places and make them seem like the norm. Or they take a school shooting and blow it into a national crisis. But the truth is that in rural communities across America you can walk down the street at any time of the day or night and be perfectly safe."

Blank looks. Can I really be telling the truth?

We talk about American movies and American television. "It's all very violent," one student says.

I can't disagree.

Eventually, I begin to see my own country from their perspective. Violence and America are becoming synonymous. What we say and do carries great weight in other countries. When Hollywood makes a movie with dozens of people killed in the space of two hours, we *lead* the world with that message.

I hope for change, but I don't expect it. For every director who makes a gentle movie, there will be several who think, probably accurately, that violence will sell out more theatre seats. For every news story featuring kindness, there will be fifty about freeway shootings, postal bombings, or some other mindless rage. How do we break this trend? Especially with freedom of speech guaranteed in our Constitution. We can't tell people to only make *good* movies and cover *nice news*.

I believe that America is changing and not for the better. We are becoming fearful. We are unlearning how to be good neighbors. It is the sadness of our age. A sadness that, I now learn, we are imposing upon the rest of the world, which is increasingly displeased with our leadership.

I started talking to these students with a Pollyanna view of my own country. I finish with a new and somewhat chilling perspective.

Under Construction

The streets of Sydney are pocked with block-sized holes. Dump trucks clog traffic. At lunchtime, men in hard hats sit on sidewalks or lean against double-parked vehicles on closed-off sections of street, eating, smoking, talking with their mates.

In an odd way, I resemble this city. There are gaping holes in my heart, my spirit. The metaphor of comparing my soul to that of a city isn't perfect but I think it is roughly appropriate.

When I left college, life seemed simple: find a job, learn to practice law, find a wife, have a kid or two, pursue the American Dream.

But it didn't work out so neatly. I bumbled through the first three years in Chelan, practicing law and learning the trade of solving people's legal quandaries. But social and dating opportunities were limited in a conservative town of 4,000 where most of the people are married and most of the bright kids have left for greater challenges in a big city.

I moved to Seattle and struggled for a year before I found an office-sharing arrangement in the sleepy suburb of Redmond. Microsoft moved to town and my practice grew. By the early nineties I was earning a good living, owned a ranch-style home in an affluent subdivision, and had a promising future.

Then my mother died in a car accident, turning my life upside down.

I was reading a novel in bed on Sunday afternoon, expecting her to arrive for a two-day visit, when the phone rang.

"Is this Robert Morse?"

I instantly knew something was wrong. The voice on the other end of the line was gravely serious. And no one has ever called me Robert, not even my father who gave me that name.

"Yes," I replied solemnly, expecting the worst. And that's what I got.

"Are you the son of Frances Morse?" And before anything more was said I knew she was gone. I put my novel down on the bedside stand and to this day I have never finished it.

She was just sixty-nine.

Much of my life had revolved around the premise that I'd always be there for her. She had never remarried. She'd taken care of my brother and me as a single mother and had made great sacrifices from the time of her divorce in 1965. I intended to repay that debt with whatever it took.

Her death changed everything.

It wasn't long before I started to question why I was still lawyering. It was stressful. I had more-or-less mastered the practice and was somewhat bored. The money was good, but I'd saved enough that I no longer felt any financial pressure. I hadn't met a woman with whom I wanted to spend the rest of my life; there were no serious prospects; the law practice certainly hadn't brought any to me.

I'd written and published a few magazine and newspaper articles. I wanted to write more. One day, I decided to quit the law and try my hand at writing full time.

I sold the suburban dream house. I closed my practice. I moved into the Chelan house I had recently inherited from my mother.

Later that year, a literary agent made a casual suggestion that I write about my wheelchair travel experiences after she heard about, and confessed that she was amazed by, my plan to go to Australia for several months.

I did some research and found no books in print about going solo, in a wheelchair, around the world. It was a perfect challenge for someone floundering in grief. I thought it might also provide opportunities to learn more about myself, and it has. I've had plenty of time to think, and I've seen plenty to *make* me think. Some of the answers are coming but it has still proven to be a slow process.

So Sydney and I have construction going on. Big time. But Sydney knows where it is headed. I still struggle with the bigger picture.

DECEMBER 3

Cairns

LEAVING INTERNATIONAL HOUSE IS LIKE LEAVING A NEW FAMILY. The kids have been so nice. A Mongolian student interrupts his morning to help me down the steep steps to the street where I'll catch my cab and then he stays around to make sure that if the threatening gray clouds to the east let loose I'll have a way to get back up the steps to shelter. It makes leaving all the more painful, this showing of concern, this love.

I'm about to tackle the first big risk of my journey. I'm to go scuba diving. I consider this as the cab transports me to the airport and I board the jet. It takes less than three hours to reach the tropics of northeastern Australia and by the time I arrive I'm no less nervous, and no less excited, about my upcoming adventure.

As I leave the jet, Cairns envelops me like a hot washcloth. The aluminum handrails on my wheelchair, cold from the baggage bay, bead with condensation and become slick. This makes it difficult to break on the long ramp while balancing the suitcase and knapsack but as usual I decline the offer of help by the gate agent. I'm still a stubborn goat. When will I learn that accepting help is okay?

The terminal is air-conditioned. Even the separate bathroom for the disabled has its own shower, a testament to how miserably hot and humid it gets this close to the Equator. As I wait outside for a cab the jungle air is redolent with a pure jasmine fragrance. I have never been any place like this.

The dispatcher is unsure which cab to put me in. I explain that my wheelchair will fit in any of them. He calls the first and watches with *The Look Of Amazement* as I swing into the front seat and pop the wheels off my wheelchair before he or the cabby can make the process more complicated by trying to help. I have stopped trying to convince people that this is much easier than it looks. Let them be amazed.

While planning this trip, I wrote to a few hotels, airlines and car companies, asking for sponsorship. In Australia, only the Holiday Inn in Cairns came through with a week's lodging.

Hotels with international names are no assurance that rooms will be well designed for wheelchairs, but the room I've been given is the most accessible one I've ever stayed in. The bathroom is large enough to easily turn the chair, with a fold-down shower bench in the corner and a hanging shower curtain and no stall, just a tile floor that gently slopes into a central drain. The sink is easy to pull up to. Even the towels are on reachable racks. The furniture doesn't block the bed. There are built-in drawers along the wall. Often, there is no consideration given to work space for a disabled person. Hotel writing desks usually aren't deep enough to keep from bumping toes on the wall, or are so high you wonder if the designer thought all guests would be at least six feet tall. But this pull-in desk is deep and wide and at a decent height. I have no problem setting up my laptop.

I'm usually hesitant to recommend a particular place, because *accessible* depends upon the needs of each person. A quadriplegic has vastly greater requirements than a paraplegic; an amputee can manage with far less. But I'd have no reservations recommending this hotel. Anyone in a wheelchair who couldn't function here shouldn't travel in the first place.

And this, by the way, has nothing to do with the fact that they're sponsoring me. That's just the icing on the cake!

The rest of the property is accessible and beautiful. A large, multi-level tropical pool with tiny waterfalls and streams, surrounded by shrubs, fills the open-air atrium. Polished granite tiles and a luxurious green carpet cover the lobby floor. Everything is spotless, no small feat in a tropical setting. And everywhere inside the building it is so very cool.

As soon as my clothes are put away, I'm anxious to locate the *Marlin Jetty* where I've been told the dive boats depart from. I find the sidewalk and head for the docks. In less than two blocks the drenching heat turns me back. I'm soaked in sweat and when I'm back in my room I take a shower, and then decide a nap is the best way to kill some time while the sun tracks across the midday sky.

When I wake up at five and head back outside, the sun is throwing long shadows from the buildings fronting the ocean on the Esplanade, Cairns' main street. It's still hot and humid and I learn this is what the climate, both day and night, is like this time of year. At least by now the sun is not beating down on the top of my head.

I am this time prepared for the heat and taking it slow and relaxed. After six blocks I stop at a place called the *Coffee Club*, an open-air cafe featuring mochas that rival Seattle's best brews, with a sidewalk patio view of the bay. Tiny waves creep up the mud flats as the tide comes in. I have fleeting thoughts of Hemingway in Cuba.

Within minutes the young woman working the espresso bar is sharing with me her poem that recently won a competition. When I ask where the dive boats depart from she points out the *Marlin Jetty*, not too distant. Then she advises where the good, cheap cafes are. I feel at home.

The setting sun paints a narrow band of pale dusky orange cloud against the ocean horizon and the bay is idyllically reminiscent of Gauguin's Tahiti. But the illusion of paradise has not always proven true.

This was the place where Captain James Cook found a way inside the Reef over two centuries ago. The discovery turned to horror when his ship become trapped and then ran aground.

It was quixotic for an English crew to sail this far, even for the promise of gold, pearls and exotic corals. Hostile Aborigines awaited them in the thick jungle, as did more species of deadly spiders and snakes (not to mention crocodiles) than any other place on earth. So Cook found himself thousands of miles from mother England and his ship was beached. After months of repairs he eventually re-floated the boat and found a channel through the *Great Barrier* and was returned to the freedom of the open ocean. Not long after that he became the victim of native spears on another Pacific island a good bit further to the north.

Down the coast is a town named *Seventeen Seventy,* after the year Cook first set foot in Queensland. That was his second Australian port of call. His first was Botany Bay.

DECEMBER 4

Great Barrier Reef

ON THIS FIRST NEW MORNING IN CAIRNS I SPRING OUT OF BED before the alarm clock stops chirping. This is the big day when I go out to the Reef.

I'm uncertain what to look for when I arrive at the buildings that front the wharf. Lights are coming on in a café and inside a man is taking chairs down from tables. I go in.

"Where's the Marlin Jetty?"

"Just out back of this building," he drones as if he's been asked this question too many times before and maybe also has a slight hangover. Once outside I follow the paved access road around the side of the complex and see that there are two long docks. Dozens of moorage slips are filled with diving and fishing boats. Two athletic-looking young men are busy arranging dive tanks on a boat but otherwise there's no activity this early in the day. The ramp is too steep and narrow to risk going out to ask for directions. I wait and wait and finally a thirty-something woman strides up carrying a regulator and a mask.

"Where's the Marlin Jetty?"

"Just over there," she says, pointing toward the second dock. "You going diving?"

"Yeah," I say proudly. "I'm going out on the Reef Endeavor."

I'm wrong. But I don't know it … yet. It's not *Reef Endeavor*, but the

60

Reef Encounter that I'm booked on for an overnight stay. The former is a luxury cruise ship, the latter a sizeable dive boat. They both came up on my Internet search for boats operating out of Cairns, and I've mixed up the names.

"Oh," she says uncertainly. "I'm not sure where they dock, but I don't think it's at the Jetty."

I know the woman on the phone said the Marlin Jetty. Still, it's only 7 AM; the boat isn't supposed to pick up divers till 7:45. I have plenty of time, but it's hard to remain calm. Still, I sense that something is wrong, but I can't quite figure out what.

"Hey!" she yells to one of the guys sorting equipment. "Where's Endeavor dock?"

"On the pier," he yells back.

She points to a long concrete pier half a mile away. "Down there." She still sounds puzzled. "Hey," she continues. "If you want some diving, I'd be glad to take you." I'm tempted to say "Yes," but I want the added adventure of a sleepover and the ship I've booked is large enough to offer overnight diving trips.

"Thanks. But I've got an overnight booked."

"Okay, well … good luck." Again, that uncertainty. My calm is rapidly vanishing.

I backtrack to the sidewalk, quickly roll down along the waterfront, shoot through an empty passage and out onto the pier. Two catamarans and a cargo ship are moored here. Nobody is around. I look for a sign, a reader board, anything to inform me I've come to the right spot. And I see absolutely nothing to give me any clue that I have come to the right spot.

For five frustrating minutes I'm alone, trying to decide what to do. Finally, a man comes strolling out of a warehouse door, lights a cigarette, looks contemplatively across the water.

"Does the Endeavor dock here?" I ask hopefully. "I'm supposed to go out for two nights and they said to meet them on the Marlin Jetty. But at the Marlin Jetty they told me the Endeavor docks here on the Pier."

"Well," he says, puzzled. "The Endeavor does dock here. But she only comes in twice a week, and tomorrow's her next docking."

Now I'm in a panic.

"I'm certain they told me they'd pick me up today," I insist. He shrugs, and I know that he must be right and I must be wrong. Could I have made such an enormous error as to write down the wrong day? "Maybe I got the name wrong," I blurt out, suddenly wanting to dash back to the Marlin Jetty. The boat is theoretically scheduled to leave in twenty minutes.

"There's a tour booth near the gas station," he says, pointing in the Jetty's direction. "They might know."

"Thanks."

I zip back through the tunnel and down the sidewalk, arriving winded and sweaty. A woman is setting up an A-frame reader board and placing an *Open* sign in the window. She sees my panic and pauses expectantly.

"I'm confused," I blurt out. "I think I'm supposed to be going out on the Reef Endeavor today. The boat I want is one hundred and twelve feet long, and I'm sure they told me they'd pick me up at the Marlin Jetty."

"You want the Reef Encounter," she says calmly. "They pick you up with a boat named Compass." She looks at her watch, then out toward the channel. "Looks like they're late. Just go out to the end of the Jetty," she points at the long dock. "You'll see it come in."

"Thanks!" I take off for the dock she has pointed to, and sure enough in a few minutes a large boat with the name *COMPASS* stenciled on the side pulls up and ties to the pilings. The people who have been milling around now quickly form a line. The man greeting passengers asks three young women in front of me for their vouchers, which they hand over. Why don't I have a voucher? Was I supposed to have made a deposit? Nobody asked me for one.

"Hi," I begin anxiously. "I'm Stan Morse and I called a month ago to reserve a spot for two nights on the Reef Encounter."

He searches the list of names on his clipboard and for a moment I fearfully imagine him saying, "Gee, I'm sorry, I don't see your name here. Who took your deposit?" But my fear is short lived.

"Here you are," he says. "Do you need a hand getting aboard?"

I'm in! "Yes," I say with relief, now eyeing the ramp and calculating just how to best make it from dock level to deck level. But the transfer becomes easy when a couple of men step up and volunteer to help me onto the *Compass* and for the first time this morning I feel relaxed.

I'm aboard with roughly fifty people, thirty-five of whom are day trippers, and fifteen of whom comprise our group of serious overnight divers.

Jeff, who checks me in, says to pick out a wetsuit.

"What for?" I ask.

"Stingers, coral, hypothermia," he replies matter-of-factly.

"Okay…." I've been told that the deadly box jellyfish don't venture out as far as the Reef. Avoiding coral seems simple enough. And the water is tepid. I don't want to seem uncooperative so early in the trip so I drag a rubber suit from the pile and drape it over a bench, wondering if I'll be able to pull on the thick, clingy rubber while sitting in my chair. I decide to worry about this later. I'm too darned glad to be on the boat in the first place to worry about some seemingly minor inconvenience like getting into a rubber suit in the tropics.

It's 85 degrees as we motor out past the headlands. The humidity hangs like a blanket and I eye my wetsuit and decide to continue to put off the torture a few minutes longer. A few of the more gung-ho types have already suited up and are now starting to look uncomfortable. My shirt comes off, then my shoes. Except for my jeans I'm now essentially naked. Why on earth are the others putting on wet suits?

My fellow divers are also now sorting through the dozens of masks and fins that are held in a large plastic tub filled with saltwater. I'm smug as I watch these obsessive-compulsive maniacs look for perfect-fitting masks. And then I realize that I'm the only one with a notebook and a pen, furiously scribbling. What kind of compulsive nut does that make me in their eyes?

As we move out the water gets clearer and bluer until it has turned to a soft sapphire velveteen and is dazzled by sun diamonds. The coastline scallops away to the south, disappearing in misty haze against the horizon.

We plough along for an hour. Those gung ho types who earlier put on wet suits have now taken them off. Several of the youngest divers who had bragged about how they stayed up late last night partying now have their heads are down on tabletops with their eyes closed.

I'm daydreaming when the engine abruptly cuts off. A crewman hurries down the aisle and lifts a hatch, scrambles down a ladder and disappears into the darkness. Up from below drifts the smell of diesel. I glance at the orange life vests hung on pegs and stuffed in open bins. I note where the closest one is and imagine my path to it, how I would put it on, which exit I'd take over the side. The image of my wheelchair cartwheeling toward the bottom flits through my mind.

From the open hatch the crewman disappeared through I can hear water sloshing between the bare metal ribs of the hull. The man finally scrambles back up the ladder, meets another crewman halfway up the aisle, and they confer in low voices. He turns on his heel and again climbs down into the ship's bowels.

Five minutes later he emerges and closes the hatch. The engine throttles up and we're again underway. He comes back and leans over the side to watch the bluish exhaust billowing from a portside vent. No explanation is given, but many sets of eyes track him with great interest as he studies the blue exhaust.

No one seems interested in napping again.

This episode now seems very *Australian* to me. The English and European expatriates who came here over two hundred years ago quickly developed a self-reliant culture in order to survive the harsh conditions of this continent. Give an Aussie a wrench and he'll fix your car. Give him a screwdriver and he'll climb down into the hold of a ship and figure a way to re-start the marine diesel. Perhaps that is an exaggeration … but perhaps not. The streak of independence in the Australians I've met is an endearing quality that I admire. It reminds me of my own stubbornly independent streak.

In another half an hour we anchor fifty yards off the *Reef Encounter*. A small aluminum pontoon boat with a Plexiglas bottom sidles up to the *Compass* and bobs nervously on the chop. Two crewmen come back to where I sit.

"How do you want to do this?" one asks. I don't really want to do it at all. It looks dangerous as hell. I look out at the surrounding ocean, then at the expectant faces of my fellow divers. I wanted adventure, right?

"Take my chair over separately. I'll grab one of you around the neck for a one-man lift. Make sure my seat cushion is down for me to sit on; I don't want to bruise my rear. Okay?"

"Let's give it a go, Mate!"

He lifts me out of my chair; another pulls the cushion I've just vacated and hands it across where it's laid on the fiberglass bench in the transfer boat. The man carrying me steps nimbly down into the small craft. There is a round of applause when I'm safely seated, but I'm sweating, and not just from the humidity. Still, I am enjoying this odd kind of celebrity.

The transfer to the *Reef Encounter* is a greater challenge since it's higher off the water, but with two crewmen carrying me we ascend the several aluminum steps to the deck while the wheelchair is passed aboard. I'm not sure who takes the deepest sigh of relief—my carriers, me, or my fellow divers—when I'm back in my chair.

The dive master, Gavin, gathers everyone in the main salon, but my chair is too wide for the doorway. "Stan," Gavin says. "I'll have a talk with you after I've filled in the others." I sit alone on the back deck, feeling left out. So much for stardom.

Catching only snatches of Gavin's presentation, I think about the next two days. This is turning into more of a challenge than I'd thought it would be. The walkways on both sides of the ship are wide enough for the chair, but one is blocked by a large equipment chest, the other by a mooring peg. I can't reach the bow. My only free access will be limited to the roughly 300 square feet of aft-deck. For meals, and to use the bathroom, I'll have to be carried inside, and the chair disassembled and reassembled. I've just glimpsed the steep, narrow stairs down into the hold, where my cabin and the showers are. I try not to think about what it will require to get me below.

After a while the engineer comes topside, spots me, and sees I'm looking a bit left out. He strikes up a conversation and I soon learn that we're aboard a *Fairmile*. This wood-hulled WWII minesweeper once had torpedo tubes, depth charge launchers and a bow-mounted anti-aircraft gun. It was designed to last five years. This ship is now fifty-two.

The meeting inside the cabin finally breaks up and divers come out and begin to pull on wetsuits and strap on tanks. Gavin squats beside me, his face filled with concern.

"What kind of injury do you have? I need to get the okay from our doctor. It's required." He shrugs.

"I'm a tee-six." I point to my xiphoid process, the small bone at the center of my chest where the ribcage ends. "I can't feel anything from here down." Gavin takes this in as if I were describing grocery purchases. Most people grimace. Good for him.

"Are you taking any medications?"

"No."

"Okay," he says. "I'll make the call and let you know."

"Don't worry," I reassure him. "I'm flexible." But I'm wondering if I'll get to dive. I sink into a quick little depression. All this way, all this effort, all this money. I wish the transfer boat were still here; I'd go back; but it's gone. I'm stuck at least until tomorrow.

The certified divers suit up and swim off in a group of eight. Gavin takes charge of the first four novices—the crewmen are calling them *virgins*—for an introductory dive.

I watch enviously from the shade on the back deck as the crewmen help nervous hands strap on tanks and weight belts. The new divers waddle down to the dive platform, grab their masks, and plunge in one at a time. Gavin waits in the water and as they plummet in he grabs them and guides them to the aluminum ladder where they clump together like grapes. I see a mixture of terror and joy on their masked faces.

He has them take several breaths through their regulators while their heads are a few inches under the surface and then they practice clearing their masks underwater. When he's satisfied no one's freaking out, he takes the group down to the bottom of the trapeze dive swing where they cluster like pollywogs. He guides them, one by one, from the swing, and they move slowly toward the coral wall.

For a while I watch the path of their bubbles trace solely along the light green zone of coral fifty yards away. Finally, I give up following their progress. I'm grumpy, sweaty, disenchanted. No one has spoken to me in twenty minutes. My depression deepens. How can the doctor do anything but reject my application? Someone should have told me to get a medical exam before I came out. This is such a waste.

I settle in to wait and my mood continues to sink. Divers and crew come and go, but they sense my sulkiness and leave me alone. One of the instructor-trainees, Geoff, finally comes over.

"How you doing?"

"I'm pretty hot."

"You want to go snorkeling?"

I hadn't even thought of that!

"Yeah," I reply. "I do."

"How can I help?"

His question is simple. But there's still a part of me that bridles at *being helped.* I'm too stubborn. How many things have I missed out on because I was afraid of being dependent in some small way? And how many people have I deprived of the pleasure of helping me? I recall my resolution to take a fresh look at myself.

"I need a couple minutes of privacy to change into my suit." I can't get to my cabin, or even indoors. Getting naked on the deck is the only way.

"Okay," he announces to everyone standing on the deck, "let's clear out so Stan can change." Three divers and a crewman move to the bow. "I'll keep an eye out," he says, then follows the others.

Getting out of jeans and into a swimsuit while trying to keep from rolling around on the deck of a ship which itself is in constant gentle motion is a real challenge. But I somehow keep from tipping over and get into my suit. When I'm ready I call out, "All clear," and Geoff returns and gives me a smile and a pat on the back. "Good on ya," he says. "Now let's get you into the water."

The stern has a four-foot-wide aluminum grate with a ladder in the middle. This is the dive platform. The aluminum is smooth so I'm not worried about scrapes, but I could easily bruise my rear. Skin breakdown is a danger to everyone in a chair. Without feeling, you don't know when you're hurt. Bruises, scrapes and cuts can become lesions or ulcers without you even knowing it is occurring.

"I need something laid on the platform to sit on," I tell Geoff. "Do you have a deck cushion?"

"No, how about a life preserver?" He points at two orange life vests. One will be adequate if I'm careful not to slip down where it splits in the middle.

Once the preserver is in place, Geoff and Jacob pick me up, carry me down the steps, and set me carefully on the preserver with my feet in the water.

I'm skipping the wetsuit. I'll take my chances with coral and stingers. The water is 85 degrees. I could stay in for hours without getting chilled.

Up to this point I've been hot, sweaty, and apprehensive. But when I roll into the water all discomfort vanishes. I use a butterfly stroke and cross toward the coral looming up from below. And here the experience of diving on the Great Barrier Reef begins. Below me is a jungle filled with coral brain clusters, forests of green antlers, delicate blue feathery antenna extending from mustard-yellow mushrooms, stretching away to infinity in all directions.

Another snorkler, Franz from Germany, swims over. "I show you something," he says. "Come." He puts his snorkel back in and swims away. I follow him over a coral wall to a pit with a sandy bottom which contains some type of mollusk which is the size of a lawnmower.

He points at his camera, at me, then at the mollusk. I nod, take the camera; he swims down in front of it and I take his picture.

I return the camera to Franz and swim away, my shadow drifting across a dream world. Small orange- and blue-striped fish play coyly among beds of waving yellow anemone. Blue surgeonfish with bright yellow tails and golden-yellow butterfly fish with black snouts parade in schools. Tiny blue cleaner fish are busily suckering every fish they can catch up to. Schools of two-inch neon-blue fish dart between the coral heads. Blue-, yellow- and white-striped angelfish eye me with scholarly detachment. Orange coral trout with turquoise spots gaze blandly up at me from their underwater paradise. A rubbery fish with body-length fins the color of ripe apricots undulates along the bottom.

But the true king of all the Reef denizens is the Maori wrasse. I see wrasse the size of wallets and wrasse the size of car tires. All with intricate dark green and brown vertical diamonds and lines covering their rectangular bodies, except on the head, where yellow and vermilion squiggles frame the gills and eyes. The large ones show no fear, coming within a few feet to see if I have food, swimming away only after they're satisfied I don't.

After twenty minutes I swim back to the ship. There are parts of the Reef I can't experience unless I can go down with scuba equipment. I want to know if Gavin has gotten permission.

It seems like forever, but Gavin finally returns with the second batch of novice divers. He climbs aboard, nods to me, and goes into the cabin to make a cell phone call.

"The doctor's given his approval," he tells me when he comes back out. "I'll take you down solo. Geoff's coming along to help. Jacob's going to lift you into the water from behind." Then he confesses that this is the first time he's taken a paraplegic on a dive. Gavin is nervous, but he's still got that *let's give it a go* Aussie enthusiasm.

They again carry me down to the dive ramp, and as my feet dangle in the water they strap on the equipment. I now discover how intimidating it is to wear a lead belt and a metal air tank with the immediate prospect of rolling forward into deep water. I shift around awkwardly on the life preserver and feel like I have lost control, as if I'm a doll with a stick for a spine and wearing a lead overcoat. Gavin tightens my straps, reminds me to breathe only through my mouth, shows me how to clear water from my mouthpiece and mask. We go over handsigns, especially the hand-flutter for trouble. I try to concentrate, to remember, but the heavy gear makes me feel like an anchor.

It's time.

"Jacob's going to lift you now," he says. "Just relax and remember to breathe." Do people actually forget to do this?

Suddenly I'm falling forward. I grab my mask with one hand as I flop face-first into the water. The tank pins me down. I'm instantly terrified of drowning.

Breathe! I remind myself. I breathe in. Out. In. Out. I have my eyes shut; I open them and see Gavin staring up at me, his face full of concern. I realize I am weightless; I can move again. I relax. Terror dissolves into fascination. I'm breathing underwater!

Gavin reaches out and takes gentle hold of me and turns me to face the ladder. I fumble to hold on as my feet try to float up and I manage to pull myself vertical with my head a few inches below the surface. Gavin's mask comes close; he signs the *OK* index-thumb circle. I sign back: *Yes,*

I'm OK. He nods and looks relieved.

The air comes easily now; I've gotten the hang of breathing through the regulator. Before I lose my nerve I want to start my first ever dive. I grab the rope and descend hand-over-hand eight feet down to the trapeze bar. Gavin sinks easily beside me, closely studying everything I do.

When I reach the bottom he flashes another *OK*, but this time with both hands, our prearranged signal. If I return it, I'm ready. But pointing up, or a flutter of my hand, means *No.*

I sign, *OK.*

Gavin gently takes my arm and I let go of the bar. For a moment it feels as if I'm dropping into an abyss, but the fear passes quickly, replaced by the amazement of actually moving around beneath the surface. We sink slowly and move off toward the coral, Gavin propelling me with one hand on my tank and the other holding my left hand. I soon realize I'm gripping his hand like a vise and I let my fingers relax.

As we descend my eardrums begin to hurt. Remembering Gavin's instruction, I pinch the plastic nosepiece and blow. The pressure vanishes. Piece of cake!

Geoff now swims into view and angles down to grab a sea cucumber off the sand that looks like a huge Tootsie Roll. He brings it to me. I take it in my hands and caress the funny animal and it feels like slick leather. I make it do a little somersault in front of me before letting it sink back to the bottom.

I had thought the water on the Reef and this far out from shore would be crystalline pure. But the Reef is instead bathed in a soup of life. Plankton. Algae. Tiny translucent shrimp. Fragments of seaweed. All sorts of flotsam fill the salt water.

We enter a long narrow coral coulee and Gavin points down. There are two ribbed clams, one the size of a microwave oven, one a little smaller, nestled in the sand. We swim to the large one, which is open about fifteen inches. Gavin motions toward it with his hand, encouraging me to reach out. I gingerly caress the smooth black flesh at the lip. The shell jerks halfway shut in response to my touch. I caress it again and the clam jerks all the way shut. I give the *OK* signal, not knowing how else to express my joy. I'm smiling so wide that water seeps in around my mouthpiece. I spit out the salty water and clamp down on the rubber with my lips, willing the smile away. My eyes are wide, my heart beating fast. This is so cool. And I'm so grateful to be here.

We shadow along a coral wall and I reach out to play tag with a tiny forest of delicate purple fronds extending from small holes. Geoff quickly swims below me and catches my legs before they can brush against the sharp coral. He and Gavin gently pull me away, and I remind myself that I know practically nothing about this world and its dangers.

I begin to experiment with up-and-down movement. At first, when I wanted to change depth, I added or let air out of my flotation vest. But now I'm taking deep breaths to rise, shallow breaths to descend. This method is both faster and far more precise.

I'm also beginning to feel a little chilled from the deeper, cooler water. I'm not wearing a wetsuit. Gavin is doing all the work pushing me around. I need to warm up. I start experimenting with a breaststroke. As my hands brush repeatedly against Gavin's equipment and body he understands what I'm trying to do. He lets go and I begin to plough through the water, clumsily at first. My legs want to sink from the weight belt around my waist, but I eventually find a rhythm to counter this. Gavin and Geoff patiently let me practice and I finally get it right, moving ahead slowly on my own.

Geoff finds another cucumber, this one with a hide of interlinked stars the size of nickels. He shows it to me and I signal for him to let it go. We pass above more giant clams. And all around us is the remarkable coral forest of every color and filled with thousands of fish.

A monster-sized Maori wrasse with magnificent green scales swims up to us, his eyes darting over out little group like a nervous puppy. He circles at ten feet, turning sideways, one eye scanning us. Gavin opens a pouch at his belt, as if to offer food. The fish darts forward and hopefully noses the flap. After finding it empty, the Wrass swims disappointedly away.

I'm getting tired, and I finally signal Gavin that I'm ready to end the dive.

As we swim toward the ship, three large Maori wrasse appear from out of the coral forest and escort us back to the hull, where they finally peel away and swim lazily back towards the coral.

"You did fine," Gavin says when we're back on the deck.

My earlier dejection is forgotten. I'm one of the gang. Not everyone made it down. One woman in her early thirties was unable to overcome her fear. I watched her earlier, hovering by the ladder. Twice she tried to let go; and twice she grabbed out in terror to regain her hold.

I'm satisfied, and hungry. I haven't eaten since morning. It's 6 PM. A few low clouds hang over the ocean. A pleasant cooling breeze has come up. The smell of stir-fried vegetables and chicken drifts up from the galley. I'm about as happy as I've ever been.

The day closes with singing. Two young women from the Netherlands, Marlais and Ingrid, are performing galley and maid chores for their board, room and diving. Both sing quite well. We start with Beatles tunes and wind up with Barry Manilow. The latter songwriter is not really a favorite of mine, but when you're wedged between two beautiful Dutch women wearing bikinis who want to sing a Manilow tune, I say you go with the flow. Under the Southern Cross, a crescent Moon, and a Venus so bright it is like a headlight, we harmonize until midnight. And when the Manilow tune brings a few catcalls from the all-guy crew, I'm not in the least bothered.

I finally run low energy and realize that it's time to face the challenges below: a toilet cubicle and a shower stall with no grab bars. Just the process of getting down below through the narrowest of stairwells is a daunting challenge.

I also must now face the possibility that I've damaged my rear while sitting on the dive platform. I haven't been alone yet, where I could reach to feel or use my small mirror to look. Even then, I could miss a problem; by morning, a welt could signal disaster.

"You ready, Stan?" Jacob asks.

"Let's do it."

Jacob and Gavin squeeze me down the narrow, steep stairwell. My elbow hangs us up for a moment as it catches where the wall makes a turn. I contort it against my chest and we get to the bottom and they take me straight to the bathroom.

"Let us know when you're done," Jacob says, leaving me on the throne with my pants still on.

I'm in a tiny cubicle with only a few inches between the walls and me. I can barely get my arms down to my sides, but somehow I manage to wriggle out of my pants. When I'm finished, inching my jeans back on is even harder. I almost fall off the stool twice. This task is further complicated by the toilet's height: it seems designed for someone six-foot-five; my feet dangle several inches off the floor.

After several sweaty minutes my belt is finally re-buckled.

"I'm ready!" I holler. They come back and hoist me up and back out into the narrow passageway. I feel relieved until we arrive at the shower stall.

I assumed they would have a plastic deck chair aboard. I could have them place it in the shower and life would be easy. No such luck. The orange life preservers are my only method of cushioning, or it is no shower at all. But I can't imagine enduring the night in the heat of my cabin with the salt of the ocean and my sweat still clinging to my body. I crave a shower and decide it's worth the risk.

The stall opens onto a tiny alcove large enough for me to disrobe in the wheelchair. That's easy. And I at least have privacy. But now I have to transfer naked onto the preservers. I pause, eying the narrow shower, on the verge of foregoing the ordeal. But the salt and sweat are beginning to make my skin crawl.

I wedge the wheelchair, as best I can, against the wall, and literally clench my teeth. There is no good pivot angle. I can't swing my rear down into the stall as I would into a tub. I inch straight forward off the chair using pure arm strength to keep from falling. The stall floor is sandpaper-rough. With no calluses, my feet are as tender as a baby's. Scraping them on the grit would flay them open. I have to make a perfectly smooth and slow transition.

Just when I've committed to going all the way, my right knee jams against the wall. I'm stuck, hanging halfway out of the chair, which now tips nervously. If it comes away from the wall it will shoot backwards, dumping me onto the floor.

I inch my rear down onto the leg rest, hoping my knee doesn't sprain as it folds like a jackknife. The wheelchair tips, teeters, and nervously settles back. Somehow it stays wedged in place. I reach out and nudge my knee; as it breaks free from the wall, my foot shoots forward. I expect to see my heel fly off the preserver and gouge across the floor. But it turns inward and miraculously stays on the preserver. I take a deep breath and settle the last few inches down onto the floor of the stall.

The two preservers continue to shift around under my weight. My legs are bent, frog-like, my knees pushed up towards my chest. I brace my elbows against the walls, then reach and slowly turn on both cold and hot water together, trying for a mix that won't burn, hoping the spray won't be too fine when it reaches me, and then the water comes strong and sweet upon my body and taking this shower suddenly seems like the best idea I've had all day long.

They've asked us to take brief showers to conserve water so after twenty seconds I shut off the water and lather up a thick shampoo. As the soap oozes down my back, the preservers become lubricated and start to shift around. But I somehow stay atop them. I turn the water back on for one precious minute and luxuriate as soap, salt and sweat disappear.

Hoisting myself back into the chair proves easy. Safely back in the alcove, I cover up with a towel, then holler, "Okay, I'm ready!"

I'm soon in my bunk, my wheelchair reassembled in the tiny room (there is no way it would have fit through the tiny cabin doorway.) I lie on the clean sheet with no thought of using the top sheet or the blanket in the sweltering heat. The tiny porthole is almost useless for air circulation. In the dark, soothed by the gentle rocking of the ship, I'm exhausted but exhilarated.

I can remember only a very few nights from my life. For instance, I remember the first night I spent away from home, in 1959, with a family that lived in a log cabin in Washington's Cascade Mountains. I also remember the night at Methodist Youth Camp, during the summer of 1966, when I first heard the Beatles' *Magical Mystery Tour* album. And there is always that pivotal night during the bleak winter of 1972 at Seattle's University Hospital when my temperature spiked and the doctors didn't expect me to live until morning.

I'll add this night to the short list.

It lasts just five hours. At first I'm kept awake by the throb of the generator and the lapping of waves against the hull. I sweat in the heat and pray for a breeze that never comes.

I'm also a little scared. Is my rear damaged? I don't want the magic of this day destroyed so I refuse to turn on the cabin's light and use my pocket mirror to check. I try not to think about it. Finally, I sleep.

I awake early, and finally concede to the necessity of taking a look. I reach back and feel each cheek. The skin is smooth! I double-check with my mirror: no redness, no welting.

I'm suddenly full of energy. I transfer to the chair, brush my teeth at the tiny sink, and dress. I'm still a prisoner inside the tiny room with no way to get up the stairs on my own. After a few tentative *Hellos?* into the small alcove at the bottom the stairs I hear a mumble from the cabin across the hall. A fellow diver sleepily opens the door to see who is calling out.

"I'm sorry," I apologize. "I was just trying to get one of the crew's attention so I could get up the stairs."

"Oh. I'll find someone." With uncombed hair and eyes pinched against the morning light he clambers up the stairs. Jacob comes back down, nursing a first cup of coffee.

"When's breakfast?"

He looks at my eager-beaver smile, shakes his head slowly. "Kids ..." is all he says.

Going back into the ocean the second day is much easier. I sit on the edge of the deck, where the experienced divers jump in, and do a neat little six-foot plunge headfirst into the water. Geoff, who has been waiting to take me down the steps, isn't quick enough to protest. I surface with a sly grin, surrounded by a fizz of bubbles, and look up for recognition of my feat. "Nice," he says disapprovingly.

Gavin and Geoff take me off in a different direction than yesterday. The only new fish I spot is a black-tipped reef shark. It's four feet long and flashes away along the bottom as soon as it sees us.

I've decided to go back to Cairns, rather than spend another night. I've seen the moon, the stars and Venus from the Great Barrier Reef. I've survived the toilet and shower. I've gone scuba diving twice, snorkeling once. It's enough. I want a long, hot, soapy shower and a restful night in a queen bed in air-conditioned luxury at the Holiday Inn. I want to savor my triumph. Most of my sixteen fellow divers will also go back today. If I stay it will be with an almost entirely new group. I'll miss the camaraderie; I don't want to be left behind.

I've spent thirty-six hours out here, being carried down halls and steps and into the galley for meals. I've allowed myself to rely upon others. In this short time, I've let loose of more control over my person than in all the twenty-six years since my accident. I've broken a wall of solitude. I finally understand how high that wall had become.

A publisher friend told me this trip would change me. I wasn't sure what she meant. But I'm seeing myself in new ways. I'm being forced to examine my weaknesses. And I'm discovering new strengths. You can easily build an emotional shell and hide inside of it when you are in a wheelchair. It takes toughness to survive. But I've just learned I can be vulnerable and still be safe. I can let people inside. It is a wonderful discovery.

December 5

A Strange Poker Game

By the time *Compass* pulls in on Friday afternoon I'm too beat to think of anything but bed. But the next night I follow up on a poker game lead.

I played some poker in college, where I learned the basic rules. But it was quarter-limit betting. The game I'll play tonight will be a lot more expensive. But the cost will be the least unusual thing about the experience.

There's a great lesson about life in poker: never expect other players to play your style. I've seen players swear and stomp away from a table because someone beat them with crummy starting cards that a good player would have folded. You play your style; let others play theirs. Accept that there are fools who play the game and occasionally get lucky. You get burned a lot less that way. It's like driving a car; never believe someone will follow your rules; always be on the defensive; always be suspicious. Pride can kill you.

Poker is all about human chemistry. One night you can play poor cards aggressively and clean up; the next night you get creamed trying to force good hands through. Players will play differently on different nights, in the same way that a wide receiver will catch the ball consistently in one game, then drop nearly every pass the next weekend. You have to pick up on the way other players are behaving and how everyone at the table interacts. No two games are the same.

Cairns' local casino is called The Reef. It's not far from the Marlin Jetty. I arrive at 8 PM, half an hour before the game is scheduled to start. The second floor is crowded with slot machines, or what the Aussies call *pokies* (for poker machines, which is apparently the most popular format.) This floor is also where the poker card-playing area is cordoned off with velvet ropes stretched between solid chrome posts. It is now empty, except for the poker pit boss, a woman in her late thirties. I go over, introduce myself, and ask about tonight's game.

"You're a bit early. No one's here yet."

"I wanted to make sure I got a seat."

"Don't worry. It usually takes a while to fill up the table. I'll put your name down."

"What games are there?"

"We have Manilla tonight."

"Manilla?"

"It's hold-em, but the cards numbered two through six are removed, so there are only thirty-two cards in the deck."

"Oh." I wish this weren't the game. I've only heard about it. Australians play it all the time. In the U.S., a full deck of fifty-two cards is the standard, and that's what I'm used to. I'll be at a great disadvantage, but I still decide to stay and try my luck.

There are two principle types of casino poker, seven-card stud and hold-em.

In seven-card stud, each player is dealt two cards face down and one card face up; then three additional cards are dealt face up to each player, one at a time, with each new card seeing a fresh round of betting. A seventh card is dealt face down. And there is one last round of betting.

In hold-em, each player receives two cards face down, and then *com-*

munity cards are turned face up in the table's center. The community cards are dealt three at the start (the *flop*), a fourth card (the *turn*), and a final card (the *river*). At each stage in the dealing there is a round of betting. The best hand is made by combining your down card(s) with the community cards, with the best five cards played as the hand.

When you take cards out of the deck, as with the Manilla game tonight, the probability of hands such as full houses or flushes increases or decreases. Only after you've played a particular game for a while do you get a sense for how often a powerful combination like a full house will come. I've never played Manilla. I have no feel for what removal of the lower-numbered cards will do to increase the frequency of power combinations.

"Are there any rules I should know?"

"You have to play both cards, and in Manilla, a flush beats a full house."

"Oh." Back home, a full house beats a flush, and you can play one or two or even no cards from your hand if the board cards are stronger.

"And we'll have thirteen players. It usually takes a strong hand, a full house or a flush, to win. You'll want to play slow until you get the hang of it."

I don't want to seem un-cool. So I say, "I'll be okay," wondering who I'm kidding. I ask the betting structure.

"Ten, twenty," she says. That means for the first two betting rounds, each player can raise ten dollars, and for the last two each player can raise twenty dollars.

I've never played in a betting structure higher than $4-$8. With thirteen players, if every player remained in the hand through every raise the pot would be $520 on just the first round. By the end of a hand, a pot in this game could exceed $1,000. It might cost me $100 to stay until the end of just one hand. I've decided that $200 is my limit to lose. It could be a short night unless I catch some good cards right off.

"And," she adds, "if there are only two players left at the end, there's no limit to the number of raises."

How would I feel if I bet four aces, and got beat by a straight flush?

I consider this information as I wander around, watching people play blackjack and roulette, wondering whether I should enter a game of this size. In the end, I decide to give it a try. After all, there's no rule requiring me to bet.

Back at the poker table a few players have arrived. I chat with two locals who play here every weekend. We talk about fishing and the weather.

Then a group of five men arrives. The pit boss apparently recognizes one of the newcomers. It's clear they aren't locals. "Introduce me to your friends," she says, and the man introduces the others by their first names.

We all sit down and the game starts. A few other players drift in and by 9 PM the table is full.

I'm seated near the center of one side of the oval table. Across the green felt sits the old white-haired guy whom the pit boss asked for introductions when he and his entourage arrived. He is bookended by two alert young men. To their left is a foul-mouthed Irishman of about forty, for whom everything is *effing* this and *effing* that. His shirt has three buttons open at the top and he wears a heavy gold chain.

The local players sit on the right end. On the far left sits a middle-aged Chinese man. He rarely speaks, but is a strong player, winning three pots in the first few minutes.

To my immediate right is a stocky fellow who resembles a well-known movie star, though clearly that's not who he is. Half an hour into the game he hasn't said a word to me, though occasionally he speaks to the fellows across the table, sometimes in Italian, sometimes in English.

The Italians, Irishman, Chinese and two other out-of-towners clearly know each other. The locals don't talk to them except as necessary for the betting.

Australian casinos are unlike American casinos in that nothing is free. They charge even for soft drinks, usually $2-$3, and hard drinks are dear in comparison to local bars. So when the pit boss announces, "Let me shout you a round, boys. Whatever you like, on the house," I'm surprised. Maybe this is a card game thing? We are, after all, a small group. No danger the casino is going to have a costly run on free booze. Still, it's unexpected.

Everyone orders. I get a heated Amaretto in a snifter. Nice.

"You boys want another, just let me know," the boss says.

Way cool.

A few minutes later a platter of sandwiches arrives. There are all kinds including ham, roast beef and turkey and with plenty of meat, fresh veggies and bread. These are not the leftovers from the end of the night when they're cleaning out the deli case. They were freshly made especially for us

"You boys want more food," she says, "just let me know. On the house."

Way, way cool.

And then I win my first hand. I'm holding four 8's, and the Chinese fellow is the only one left. We bet, raise, raise again, and he finally calls. I expose my cards and he grimaces, then throws his cards into the muck (the term for all discarded or unused cards.) The fellow to my right leans over and quietly says, "Good on ya Mate, ya beat the Chink."

I'm not racist. I've never felt any animosity towards another race.

And it bothers me when someone makes a statement like this. But what am I supposed to do? There's nothing *to do*, except say, "Thanks."

I rake in over $300, and now I'm up in the game and feeling pretty good. While the dealer is shuffling, I turn to the fellow who made the comment.

"I'm Stan," I say, holding out my hand. "Nice to meet you."

He smiles, shakes my hand, gives me his name. It's very Italian.

"You from here?" I ask.

"No." He's mildly perplexed at my question.

"What do you do?"

Again, that puzzled look, and he mumbles, "I own nightclubs," and he looks down at the cards he's been dealt.

A great flash of comprehension comes to me. Out-of-town Italians. Free drinks. Free food. Beating *the Chink*. Owns nightclubs. My hands feel cold as I check my two cards.

I play for another hour and gradually lose back what I've won and then go in the hole for roughly $100 by the time I leave. Never have I been so happy about losing money in a poker game.

Later I describe this night to a journalist friend.

"Have you any idea who you were playing with?" he says incredulously.

"Nope," I reply. "And I don't want to know. They were pleasant. It was fun. End of story."

DECEMBER 15

Small Disasters

BEFORE LEAVING CAIRNS I BUY A BOTTLE OF SOUTHERN COMFORT as a gift for Gavin. He said it was his favorite. I want to surprise him with this special thank you for making my dives happen. I leave repeated messages on his answering machine but he never calls back.

I'm not a whiskey drinker, but it cost $30 and I'm reluctant to throw it away. I consider leaving it at the hotel desk and asking them to call Gavin, but liquor delivery is low on the favor totem pole. They've already done enough. I decide to take the bottle with me in my backpack.

On the morning of my departure I'm excited about traveling to Brisbane on the *Sunlander*, reputed to be one of Australia's premier train experiences. Trains were the lifelines to outlying bush regions in Australia's early days. On a continent as large as the U.S., but with a tiny population, highways were a luxury. Unfortunately, there was no national track gauge standard. In the old days passengers switched to a new train at each state border because the track in the neighboring state was of a different gauge. The railway coaches were also different in their construction, some spacious, some tight-quartered.

Today there is a single gauge of track, but the uniqueness of the cars has sometimes survived. Unlike Amtrak in the U.S., *accessible* doesn't always mean the same thing in each of Australia's states.

My sleeper car turns out to be not accessible by any standard. The wheelchair won't even fit through the door to the outside. Instead, they'll cart me on in a transfer chair that looks like a flimsy baby stroller. Worse, the bathroom isn't attached to the room, it's down a narrow hallway. So for thirty-one hours I'll have to call a conductor every time I need to use the bathroom. A shower is impossible. And finally, I'll have to share the tiny room with another passenger. I imagine a smoker who snores.

In the tepid humidity of early morning, standing with the pressure of boarding a large crowd beginning their summer holidays, the porter grows agitated with my indecision. This is the man who will be taking me to the bathroom in the middle of the night and he seems none-too-pleased at the prospect, though he doesn't say it directly. I decide to bail out of this experience. Sometimes it is better to face the reality of a situation. I roll over to where the porter is waiting for my answer.

"Can I get my ticket refunded?"

"I think so. Go ask at the office." He turns his full attention to the other first-class passengers waiting to board.

The office promises to credit my Mastercard and takes the necessary information. I catch a cab to the airport. The Ansett flight ends up costing the same as the train ticket.

As I'm boarding, I leave my two bags, the knapsack containing most of my clothing and the Southern Comfort and the suitcase containing my laptop computer, at the end of the jetway. I tell the fellow loading me with an aisle chair that I need both bags inside the cabin and he agrees to make sure they follow me in.

I'm in my seat and I wait for the bags. Boarding continues. No bags. All of the passengers are finally on. The captain announces we'll be leaving shortly, that we should fasten our seatbelts. Still no bags.

I waive frantically to a flight attendant, who hurries down the aisle to see what my emergency is.

"Yes sir?"

"I need my two suitcases. I've got a computer in one and it can't go into the hold. You've got to find them for me!"

"I'll get them Sir. But could we store them up front? There's not enough room in the overhead bins."

I hand-carried both bags on the flight up to Cairns and they fit easily in the bins. I'm on the same type of plane. I know they fit. But I don't care, as long as they're inside and the computer is safe. A replacement would cost $3,000 plus two weeks of waiting for it to be shipped from Seattle with my software.

"Sure," I say. "You can put them anywhere inside. Just don't let them go below!"

The attendant returns shortly with bad news. The bags are already stowed in the main hold. There's nothing he can do.

I figure the odds are high that my computer won't survive. And I'm really mad, mostly at myself, for letting the bags out of my sight.

When we arrive in Brisbane I demand that one of the agents at the gate accompany me to the luggage carousel. I want no doubt about who is responsible if the computer has been destroyed. I tell him the airline can buy a replacement computer, since I explained in Cairns why the bags needed to come in with me.

I pull the computer out of the suitcase and flip the power switch. It runs. I feel ridiculously lucky. I thank the agent and then catch a cab into the city. I have completely forgotten the Southern Comfort bottle in my other bag.

My Aussie cabby is an old-timer determined to find me an accessible room at a bargain price. Occupancy rates have remained extremely low, even though it's summer. Because of the monetary crisis, the Koreans and Japanese haven't come; last year they came in droves. I have plenty of options. But the first three we stop at don't have accessible rooms.

"This one's pretty good," he says, pulling into a Travelodge. "And it's right next to the train station." I've told him I must catch an early XPT train to the Hunter Valley in four days' time. He goes inside, returns.

"They've got a disabled room, Mate, but it's only open for one night. What do you think?"

"I'll take it." I'm tired. I want a shower. I want to put the stress of almost losing my computer behind me. It turns out to be a very nice room.

As I unpack, I discover that the Southern Comfort bottle that was in my backpack has shattered. My clothing is saturated with liquor. The two shirts wrapping the bottle are imbedded with glass slivers. I drop them into the garbage. It's now officially a bad-hair day.

Later, I talk to the manager about room availability for the next three nights. She says they have several vacant rooms, they just aren't handi-capped-designed. After my experience of showering on the *Reef Encounter* I feel silly insisting on a fully accessible room. I tell her I can shower in the tub. She suggests I look at a king suite on the top floor.

The room I'm shown is big enough to throw a dance party in. She offers it at the same price as my smaller room, the equivalent of $65 US. I take it.

The following morning the newspaper headline reads: *DENGUE FEVER BREAKS OUT IN CAIRNS*. It's the rare Type 3 strain that causes hemorrhagic bleeding. Mosquitoes along the Esplanade have infected dozens of people. I spent many evenings on the Esplanade. I seems that I left just in time.

ON MY LAST FULL DAY IN BRISBANE I HAVE A CHANCE ENCOUNTER at the reception desk with a flight attendant whose crew is checking out and, ever the self-promoter, I tell her about my book project.

"Are you going to New Zealand?"

"Why?"

"I fly for Air New Zealand."

"I'll be there in January."

"What part?"

"I fly into Christchurch and then go to the north island to Lake Taupo for some fishing."

"Well," she says, taking out her card and writing a number on the back, "my husband and I have a house on the southern shore of Taupo. Give us a call when you get there. We do lots of fishing in the summer, maybe we can help."

Sometimes you have to be willing to create your own luck.

DECEMBER 19

Wine Country

I DETEST GETTING UP EARLY. I REMEMBER BEING SIXTEEN AND rising at 5 AM to thin apples and set irrigation line. I was barely drying my hair each morning when the sound of grinding gears would signal Rick's ancient Willy's Jeep coming up our hill. We clocked eight hours in Bill Wild's orchard before the mid-afternoon temperatures hit the high nineties.

The XPT train to the Hunter Valley leaves at 6:30 AM. Setting the alarm for 4:45 conjures that teenage memory, and also my recent Los Angeles airport ordeal. I crave sleeping in. Only bakers and parents with small children should be required to rise this early.

It takes me a longer time to shower and dress, usually a full hour. And when you're in a wheelchair, you learn to also arrive a few minutes early, just in case they don't expect a wheelchair and there's a problem making the accommodation. Even so, I sleep a few extra minutes. The station is only a five-minute walk away.

Finally, I struggle up, shower, dress and pack. Longing for coffee and breakfast, I drop my key at the desk. I'm starved, and train food is … train food.

Joining other sleepy-looking travelers on platform one, I read the paper while we wait for the conductors to open the cars. It's Christmas holiday and the train is full but the people on the platform are relaxed in typical Australian fashion. If there's Christmas stress it's hard to detect.

Unlike the Sunlander the XPT has a handicapped bathroom at the end of the first-class cars. There's also a small fold-down table for wheelchair travelers at the back of the car. I can't roam the train because the aisles are too narrow but it won't be an uncomfortable trip with the bathroom and workspace amenities.

The train is scheduled to stop briefly at the small town of Maitland, in the Hunter Valley, at 7 PM. Norm Topp of the Hermitage Lodge, where I'm staying for the Christmas holiday, promised to meet the train.

Just south of Brisbane the train climbs into a range of rounded mountains. The worn canyons are filled with lush ferns and grasses and sprinkled with eucalyptus and a few pines. At one bend in the track I spot three huge gnarled willows that overhang a shallow creek which runs and pools over smooth bedrock. I imagine pioneers who must have planted them as a reminder of the land they left, probably England. It is a romantic little spot that now disappears from view but it must have been a difficult place to live and farm because no one remains upon the old homestead.

We leave the hills after two hours and emerge onto the vast pancake flatness of the coastal plain. The tropical humidity of the north is now gone. Except for occasional pastures where cattle and sheep graze, the land is covered with a sparse forest of various eucalypts, mostly box and gum trees. There has been a drought here for many years and the underbrush is kindling-dry. The trees look exhausted with their yellowing leaves and drooping branches. Bush fires have been burning this summer throughout Australia.

Occasional huge stumps testify to the great forest which once grew here. Now there are only smaller trees, many just saplings: the legacy of clear-cutting.

Less than an hour out of Maitland, a hopeful sprinkling of rain streaks the windows. A massive thunderhead climbs against the western horizon. Lightning lashes from the billowing gray mass of clouds. When the train pulls into the tiny brick station the air is cool but the storm has already passed to the west. The cool air is a welcome relief from the extreme heat which has characterized this summer.

I sit in front of the station, alone with my two bags, swatting at the ubiquitous black flies that come with summer in this country, wondering if something has happened. Maybe I gave the wrong arrival time in my letter? My worry is short-lived. A blue van veers off the road and into the parking lot and Norm's balding head is behind the wheel.

"Sorry," he says as he loads my bags. "It's been busy." I assure him I've only been here a few minutes. I remind myself that Norm has two small boys, a marriage, a lodge, a restaurant, and grape vines to look after.

I've looked forward to visiting Norm and Helen Topp. Last summer I stayed at their small resort. We hit it off immediately and I was treated like a family member. Helen and the boys took me at dusk one evening to see my first wild kangaroos. When Norm went on errands I was always invited along. Before a busy night in their gourmet restaurant, *Il Cacciatore*, we would often sit and sip a glass of wine or a cappucino, sharing travel experiences and speculating about what we each might be doing the following year.

"It's hot," I remark, as we drive up through the rolling hills. It seems that with each mile further inland we gain another degree. The radio tells us it's 32 degrees (88 degrees F) in nearby Newcastle. The van has no air conditioning and the humidity and heat have plastered my shirt to my back and chest.

"It got up forty-three two days ago," Norm says, as the van rocks down the narrow road. Norm drives as if he's left a pie baking and wants to get back before it burns. I try to ignore this while I do a quick temperature conversion. I figure that 43 degrees C is 108 degrees F!

"Forty-three?"

"Yeah. Everyone was worried about the grapes. The vines needed a rest. But it's been cooler the last couple days. We've had a little rain. But it's supposed to get hot again."

My room at the lodge has air conditioning and it seems like I'll get a lot of writing done, venturing out only after dark to eat in the restaurant and to admire the southern stars, particularly the Southern Cross.

I'm spending Christmas with Norm, Helen and their sons Sam (6) and Alex (3). It's been years since I've spent Christmas around children. I hope this will prove a distraction for what has always been a tough time of year for me.

When I was a kid, Christmas was a time to be reminded of tight finances. We were fortunate if the mortgage was current and the oil tank was full. When other kids came back to school talking about Disneyland or Hawaii or new bikes or train sets, I could report only a new sweater, a shirt, perhaps shoes. I kept quiet and usually no one asked.

This is also the time of year when I broke my back.

I hate having a sour holiday season attitude and I hope this year will be different. I've even done a little preparation. After a long search for something I could ship ahead, I bought several knitted finger puppets for the boys. They were the only gifts I could find which were light enough to include in my luggage. I'm told they're popular this year but I remain nervous about giving gifts. Will they like them? I hate the apprehension of somehow failing to please kids at Christmas time.

I had similar fears when it came to presents exchanged between me and my mom. We were usually on different wavelengths. Mom would pick out an onyx pen set, a brass music box, or a garish tie. And I invariably gave her perfume or a scarf she wouldn't have chosen for herself. We had some great laughs about this and it never damaged our relationship, but it always perplexed us when a gift was called for.

Occasionally I got it right. The strand of pearls was my best guess. She had always insisted jewelry was an unnecessary luxury, but the expression on her face when she opened the flat box and saw the large white orbs told a completely different story.

Some things you cannot escape. I've come this far, but Christmas, and my feelings about the day, remain a constant. At least it's warm. And I have a family to be with.

Christmas

THE NEXT MORNING, SIX-YEAR-OLD SAM KNOCKS ON MY DOOR AT 7:00 AM. I open it a crack, not yet dressed.

"Can you come watch us slide on the grass?"

Behind Sam, his younger brother Alex clutches a square of cardboard. A towhead blond, he flashes an innocent grin which is impossible to deny.

I've already heard Helen caution them not to bother me but I've encouraged their friendship and I'm glad they're comfortable coming to see me.

"I'd love to, Sam. But I've got to shower and get dressed. Can you come back in half an hour?"

"Okay."

Alex beams. He and Sam tromp off towards the grass.

As I shower and dress, I'm quite pleased that the boys have included me in their lives. Kids have the best sense of when someone truly cares and they can be generous when it comes to love.

When I go outside, I discover that Sam has scavenged a long, sturdy box from the restaurant. He climbs in, beating flat the stiff corners as he tumbles down a grassy bank for about thirty feet. Alex contents himself with sliding toboggan style on his square of cardboard. When they reach the bottom, they shout: "Watch this one!" Then scramble back up and recklessly try to out-do each other.

After fifteen minutes of watching from the building's deck I'm suffering from the heat, even with a cap and sunglasses and sitting in the shade. I'm also concerned one of the boys will get hurt trying to impress me. "Boys!" I holler. "Let's go inside."

We go into the empty restaurant and sit at the espresso counter, the boys' legs dangling from the bar stools. We talk about the toys Santa might bring.

In a few minutes Helen appears and shoos them out to play, then makes us lattes. "I hope they don't drive you crazy," she says, handing me a mug.

"They're great. I don't think they could ever drive me crazy."

Her brow rises and her brown eyes say, *You've got to be joking.* "Give them a chance," she says in an amused voice.

The Hunter Valley is a coal-mining region. Its principal city, Newcastle, was named for the famous English coal-mining town. The area also has a wine industry dating from the turn of the century. Shiraz and Chardonnay thrive in the hot summers and mild winters. A recent explosive growth in the wine market has brought an increasing number of boutique labels to join the few large vintners. Wine tours have become all the rage for Sydneysiders wanting a weekend escape from *The Big Smoke* (Sydney's nickname).

It's still two months before the harvest and the wine release parties that will draw the wealthy from Sydney and beyond. The grapes are green and hard as peas. But the tasting rooms are open.

On my third day I take a tour, ignoring a predicted high of over 100 degrees. As I board the twenty-seat coach at 10:15 AM it is 90 degrees. The bus is air-conditioned, but most of the tasting rooms we will visit have only ceiling fans.

The twelve people already aboard are fascinated as I swing from my wheelchair onto a pillow on the first step, lift myself onto a second cushion on the coach floor, and boost myself up to a seat. I get a small round of applause. Compared to dive boat transfers, this is easy, but I still relish the attention.

I once tried to *drink my money's worth* on an Australian wine tour. Big mistake. The tour lasted seven hours. Wineries here don't skimp on their samples. I was miserable by the end. Today, I stick to sipping reds and drinking plenty of water.

By mid-afternoon it's 105 degrees. "Dry heat," someone says.

"Yeah, like my kitchen oven. And I don't climb in there!" I reply.

You hear stories when you travel. Charlie, a Canadian teacher, is also circling the world, but in the direction opposite to mine. He is a gifted storyteller and entertains the group with anecdotes about Europe and Asia. And warnings the like of which I've not yet heard.

"Be sure to leave the window of the railcar open if you travel overnight in Italy," he says.

"Why?"

"They gas you by sliding a tube under your door. You wake up with a headache, and not much else."

This seems unlikely. But … .

People on the tour gather close to hear Charlie's stories. It is cool in the cellar and we are not anxious to go back out to the hot bus. Charlie tells us a series of tales.

"In Bali they have a trick where someone comes up and asks for change. When you make change, two guys come up claiming they're policemen and accuse you of doing a drug deal. When you protest they demand to see your money. The guy who is setting you up hurriedly hands them his money, they inspect it, and give it back. Then they take your money, and when they give it back it's not all there."

I promise the people in our group, who seem quite concerned about my safety for the remainder of my adventure, never to make change for anyone or to go overnight on a train in Europe without leaving the window open a crack.

His strangest and most frightening story actually happened to him in Bali.

Early one morning, he met a well-dressed older gentleman who said his daughter was shortly to graduate from college and had decided to go backpacking in Canada for her graduation gift. He asked Charlie to talk to her and give her some tips. The man seemed quite sophisticated, and Charlie agreed. He invited Charlie to his home to meet the daughter.

Charlie became suspicious when the trip took an inordinately long time, winding through several back streets, before reaching a nice house. The daughter, Charlie was told, would be home soon.

Shortly thereafter, a very excited fellow in his twenties, whom the man identified as his son, arrived. He told Charlie there was a rich American woman who wanted to play high-stakes blackjack and she was on her way, at that very moment, to the house. The son told Charlie he could manipulate the cards and trick the woman out of her money, but he needed a partner. Was Charlie interested? The son was insistent, and offered Charlie a percentage of the winnings. He showed Charlie how the trick worked. Charlie felt he was in some danger, so he decided to go along until he could devise a safe way to leave.

A woman in her mid-forties arrived within a few minutes. She sounded American, though a few words weren't quite pronounced correctly. After introductions, a game was set up, with Charlie as the bank, the woman playing against him, and the son as dealer.

Initially, things went according to plan. The woman dropped several thousand dollars. In frustration, she finally blurted angrily: "I want to play one last hand for fifty-two thousand dollars!"

"Of course," the son agreed readily.

"I need to know you can pay if you lose," the woman insisted. "I need to see your money." The son looked surprised, and asked for a moment to talk to his partner. He then took Charlie into the next room.

"I don't have that much money here," he said painfully. "Do you have some money? We have to cover this bet. We can make a killing!"

"No, I don't have that kind of money." Charlie now understood what the scam was. No way was the woman going to lose her last bet and it would be she the son was splitting profits with, not Charlie.

The son grew angry.

"You must have some money. You can get an advance on your credit card. This is a sure thing! But we need to show her the cash!"

"I don't have that kind of money!" Charlie was telling the truth. But he was also very scared. He had heard stories of tourists being beaten, even killed, by con artists. If he could just get away from the house he might be safe. "If you take me back to my hotel I can arrange something," he said, hopefully.

"Okay," the son quickly agreed. "I'll take you."

They returned to the woman. "We don't have that much cash here," the son told her. "But Charlie can get it at his hotel."

"Okay, I'll wait." She sounded as though this had been expected.

As soon as they reached the hotel Charlie said he could not get cash, and that the son should leave or Charlie would call the police. The son stormed out of the lobby.

Charlie thought this was a unique occurrence, until he related the incident to a fellow traveler. The man said, "I've heard of them. An American lost thousands of dollars to that group three days ago. You're lucky."

Charlie is like an inoculation: he reminds me that not everywhere I plan to travel will be safe.

I survive the wine tour. The days melt away.

On Christmas Eve, Norm and Helen have me over for dinner. Sam and Alex run full-tilt all evening, energized by the prospect of opening presents the following morning. Finally, Helen declares bedtime. The boys resist until she reminds them that Santa can't deliver presents while they're awake.

The next day the boys thank me for the finger puppets, but they seem more interested in the mechanical toys. Dump trucks, bulldozers, toy guns. It's okay. I'm included in their lives, like an uncle, and it's more than enough. For the first time in years I enjoy Christmas.

DECEMBER 27

A Friendly Bus Driver

THE BUS TO SYDNEY LEAVES MID-AFTERNOON FROM CESSNOCK'S
deserted main street. I wait in the sweltering heat with four other passengers in the narrow shade thrown by a two storey building. The previous summer I was fortunate on bus travel from here. Les Curtis, the coach driver, carried me on and off the bus. He was even humorous about it. "Give us a cuddle," he said, and cradled my legs as I put my arm around his neck.

Today, I haven't a clue who will be driving.

I can get out of my wheelchair the way I did on the wine-tour bus. But that was just two small steps. Here, there are three large steps and a high seat and I've no cushions or blankets to put down on the steps to protect my skin. The risk is much greater.

A large bus with tinted windows finally lumbers into view, edging with a squeal of hydraulic brakes to a stop at the curbside. The door hisses. And out steps my old buddy Les!

"What're you doing here?" he says, surprised.

"I came south on the train."

"Been drinking a bit of wine, I imagine."

"I imagine."

"Well, wait until I've got the others on, then you can give me a cuddle." He smiles and begins taking tickets from the short line of waiting passengers. After he's finished with them he carries me aboard the bus.

"How've you been?" he asks, as we pull out of Cessnock.

"Great." I describe my trip.

"I'm sure you'll want to write all about the best bus driver you've ever met. Be sure you spell my name right," he says jokingly, then hands me a card. *Nothing but Trains* it says, listing him and his wife Pam as owners. So then we talk about trains and my plan to take the *Indian Pacific* between Adelaide and Perth.

Three hours later, Les deposits me at Central Station in Sydney.

DECEMBER 28

Mozart at the Opera House

SYL'S HOMESTAY IS BOOKED FULL AND I'M THANKFUL TO HAVE a room. Friends from as far away as South Africa have come for Paul and Syl's twenty-fifth anniversary and a renewal of wedding vows.

On December 28 the small crowd of celebrants gathers at the Rose Bay dock and piles onto the private ferry *Radar* to begin a lazy three-hour circuit of the harbor. We are soon all drinking champagne, eating smoked salmon and giant shrimp, and listening to a Dixieland jazz band. As I shovel down crab canapés I silently promise to resume a healthy diet in New Zealand.

Paul and Syl are friends of Greg Lenthen, the travel editor for the *Sydney Morning Herald*. He and I have been exchanging email for weeks. I've been trying to interest him in commissioning a piece on wheelchair travel. He's here for the celebration, and we finally meet in person. As we talk, the *Radar* chugs by the Sydney Opera House.

"Have you been to the opera yet?" Greg asks.

"No. I've wanted to. I just haven't found the time."

"You should go before you leave."

"I'd love to, but I head out for New Zealand in four days."

"Mozart's Cosi Fan Tutte opens on New Year's Eve."

"I'd never get a ticket this late." I've checked; it was sold out. Even my wheelchair couldn't get me in.

"Call the publicist," Greg says matter-of-factly. "Tell them you're a journalist. Use my name if you want."

"Really?"

"Sure. They need good publicity. And you'll reach a market they don't advertise in. I'll call you tomorrow with the number."

"Great!"

When I call the next morning, there's instant suspicion in the Assistant Publicist's voice. I describe my project, mention Greg's name. She says they're booked solid for the New Year's Eve gala. The "I'll see if we can do something" comment seems merely a courtesy.

The morning of New Year's Eve I take the *Dawn Fraser* jetcat into the city. As we glide past rugged old docks, piers, and parks with grassy banks that run down to the water, I can see people already setting up chairs to watch the night's fireworks. I decide not to return for the fireworks and brave the expected crowd of over one million. Normally, crowds don't bother me, but one this large, comprised of New Year's revelers many of whom are bound to be inebriated, seems a bit too much of a gamble. Aussies can get a bit crazy. Give them a chance and they'll drink you under the table, then they'll climb up and dance on that table!

When I return to Syl's at 2 PM, I learn the Australian Opera has called: a ticket will be waiting for me at the press desk. Call me fickle, but this changes everything. A free ticket to what is arguably the world's most famous opera house? The rowdy crowd is forgotten.

But now I've got a new problem. My best clothes consist of a long-sleeve blue dress shirt and khaki pants, which are far from adequate for the opera. Are there clothing stores open on New Year's Eve? Unlikely. Maybe I can find a seat in the back of the hall where no one will notice my ragamuffin appearance? Being in a wheelchair, they'll probably cut me some slack and at least let me in. But I hate the thought of making a bad showing, especially as a guest journalist. I don't want it getting back to Greg that I showed up in work clothes.

Even though I expect no clothing stores to be open, I decide to make a search for clothes anyways. So I take the 4:06 jetcat back into the city and roll away from Circular Quay into the heart of downtown. After a hot uphill climb I'm sweating profusely and I've seen nothing that looks remotely like a men's clothing store.

I take a right and go two more blocks. Still nothing. I decide to return to the waterfront before I'm entirely drenched in my own sweat, hoping they at least sell ties at the Opera House gift shop.

One block from the Quay I get truly lucky when I discover a tiny men's shop that is still open. The Lebanese owner listens patiently to my plea for help and then he fusses like a loving uncle to fit me in black cotton pants. He selects a silk tie and knots it around my shirt collar. "There," he says, stepping back to admire his work. "You look terrific."

Half an hour later, I'm at the Opera House. My ticket is waiting at the press desk. A security guard escorts me through the Green Room, where the costumed cast is chatting and snacking on finger sandwiches.

Through a side door and now we're in the main reception hall where all of the men are snazzed up in colorful tuxedos. I feel like a street urchin despite my new duds, but the wheelchair turns a small miracle; a lovely woman in an ornately sequined gown sees me, walks over.

"Would you like something to drink?"

"Yes, thank you. Some champagne?"

"I'll get you a glass."

"How much is it?"

She *poo-poos* this question with a raised eyebrow. "You wait here," she says, and quickly returns with a flute of bubbly.

"To Mozart!" I offer.

"Cheers!" She takes a sip. "You're an American?"

"Yes."

"What brings you to Sydney?"

I tell her of my travels. She's fascinated, and I'm suddenly adopted into her social circle. She introduces me to several friends, then to her husband, who has returned from parking the car. The coterie listens intently and offers congratulations before shifting to gossip about the cast: who is seeing whom, who did what to whom, etc.

When the lights dim to signal us inside, she hands me a CD. "A present to remember Sydney by," she says. It's the musical score for tonight's performance.

That easily, I am part of a night at the opera.

The production is wonderful. Incredible costumes, great voices. The hall has a gentle brilliance, a charming intimacy. There is no dark recess for me in the back of the hall. Instead, I'm in the fifth row, in a perfect wheelchair space.

We break after dark has fallen and go out to watch a special display of early fireworks. There is a space cordoned off for opera patrons, which is a good thing, because all of Sydney has come down to the waterfront. For the next forty-five minutes we watch as a million dollars worth of pyrotechnics go up in starbursts directly in front of us.

We return for the second act of the opera. After the finale, a shower of balloons comes cascading from above and the audience throws volleys of colorful streamers which we have been handed by the ushers. Near midnight the final curtain drops.

With confetti streaming from my spokes, I race through the crowd outside. The Quay rail station is now almost vacant, but in just an hour, after the midnight fireworks display, it will be jammed. I catch the Bondi Junction train and then get a cab to Syl's.

JANUARY 3

New Zealand

I ARRIVE IN CHRISTCHURCH, NEW ZEALAND AT 1:30 AM ON one of the few flights that come direct from Sydney. By the time I've cleared Customs, caught a cab and checked into the hotel, it's 3 AM. I'm not making the same mistake I made in L.A. by trying to stay up all night and save the cost of one night's lodging. Besides, with the favorable exchange rate, $60 U.S. buys a fully wheelchair-accessible deluxe room at a four-star hotel.

Christchurch turns out to be a sanitary city of around 350,000 with a distinctly country feel. The central district is compact and flat and only a handful of buildings exceed ten stories. The most thrilling experience in the downtown area seems to be the romantic Florence-style gondolas which cruise the placid river meandering through the park. Otherwise, there are daytrips into the countryside in every direction. A fleet of immaculate tour busses rules the uncongested streets. Christchurch seems like a wonderful place to honeymoon.

I'm bored out of my mind by sunset of the first day.

It affects my writing. I have no profound thoughts and come up with nothing even hinting at adventure. The Barrier Reef and Sydney are a hard act to follow.

On Saturday night I visit the local casino and play Caribbean stud poker. It's not that I particularly like the game, but there's nothing I find more interesting, no real poker, no craps, just blackjack and slots. Strangely, I win, and by midnight I'm up $250. I cash in my chips and return to the hotel.

On the afternoon of the second day I meet a street vendor, Murray, at an outdoor crafts fair. He is selling wooden bowls and boxes, and when I lament about not finding a fishing guide he says he'll ask a friend of his to take me fishing.

When I reach my room that evening the phone light is blinking red. Murray has left a message to call him in the morning. I'm excited, convinced my fishing adventure is a done deal.

I drag myself out of bed early the next day and dial Murray's number. He apologizes and says his fishing buddy has gone away for several days and won't return before I leave. He instead gives me a local guide's name and number. It's Sunday, and he says I must wait until Monday to call.

I thank him and leave the impression that I'll follow up, but I know I won't. I've already contacted several guides on the Internet and by phone. Only one was interested in wheelchair anglers, and that was solely for lake fishing and he was asking a small fortune. The stream-fishing specialists wanted nothing to do with carting me around. They mentioned rates of several hundred dollars per day, and if a helicopter was involved it was over a thousand. For a few fish?

Sunday turns out to be my only decent day in Christchurch. After that, things go haywire.

On Monday, I return from lunch, insert my card key, and the light flashes red. I go downstairs, and the manager re-programs the card. Back up to the tenth floor, and the lock still shuts me out. A fear blossoms that they've re-let my room and now my cameras and computer are gone. I storm down to the lobby. The manager comes up with her master key, opens the door, and to my relief everything's still there.

That evening, as I fiddle under the table to plug my computer into the phone jack, my back rocks the table, the lamp tips over, and the glass shade shatters. I spend ten minutes picking splinters off my lap, legs, the floor and my computer, greatly relieved that I'm not cut. Why is the shade made of glass in the first place?

Next, I'm unable to get onto the Internet. My modem won't accept the dial tone. I pray it hasn't been fried and that it's the phone system's fault. Remembering the *X3* command I used to get it to work in Australia, I wonder if erasing that line of code will help. I decide to try this. Perversely, I can't find the screen where I typed in *X3*. I feel incredibly stupid.

The next day the computer mysteriously logs onto the Internet on my first try. It stays on five minutes, then just as mysteriously disconnects. I try to get back on, but the modem is again on the blink. Or is it the phone system? No clue. I have the urge to throw my computer against the wall.

I glare at the unresponsive Netscape screen for two minutes before realizing that I need to settle down. During my brief connection I was at least able to collect my email. I count my blessings. No one has died, my house hasn't burned, the newspaper received my last story.

Part of my problem with Christchurch is mobility. There's no light rail. Cabs are expensive. Much of the city is residential and spread out. To find adventure I need to get out of town, but the only options are tour busses, and I'm not quite ready to sink to that level.

I wish I'd brought my portable hand controls. They're simple enough: two steel rods, one bolting to the brake, the other to the gas. Even in a left-lane country, where drivers sit on the right, they should work on rental cars. Unfortunately, it would take a week to have the controls air freighted to me. I don't even consider trying to find a rental car with hand controls already installed. Handicapped equipped rental cars are hugely expensive, if you can find one at all.

My misfortunes continue.

The frames of my sunglasses have somehow become bent. I can't find an optician who will fix them, and replacing them would cost $150. Why are decent sunglasses so expensive? I decide to wait until I return to Australia, where I'm certain I can get them fixed, or where I can find a cheap replacement.

The weather even turns against me. The day I arrived it reached 100 degrees and was the hottest day in ten years. I sunburned my lips and now they're chapped and painful. The ozone hole seems worse here than in Australia. The second day, it barely heats up into the low 60's. A cutting wind blows up from the arctic sea. I freeze in my T-shirt, but sweaters are more expensive than sunglasses. In six days I'll be back in sweltering Australia. I've no luggage space for heavy clothing. I'm unwilling to buy a sweater that I'll have to throw away in less than a week.

I finally bite the tour-bus bullet and ask the concierge to look into options for going to Hanmer Hot Springs, a thermal resort two hours up into the mountains. He reports back that the bus isn't wheelchair-accessible. He also cautions that the summer season in Hanmer is very busy and lodging might be difficult and even if I can find something available the rooms are expensive. The country hotels and lodges are of older construction and most have steps. There's no guarantee of a handicapped-accessible room being available. I reluctantly strike Hanmer from the list.

I finally decide to leave Christchurch early and head up towards the northern island. I check out the train and am told my wheelchair will have to be stowed with the luggage. I tell the agent this is ridiculous; there must be some way I can keep my chair. The trip takes all day. I'll have to call the porter to use the bathroom, and endure the torture of being carted around in whatever they use to move disabled passengers. I imagine my chair being stolen, unloaded at the wrong stop, or simply lost. He won't yield.

I decide to fly. I'll miss the ruggedly wild and beautiful eastern coast. I accept this, reminding myself that I came here to fish, not sightsee.

All flights to Lake Taupo are full, so I settle for Wellington, which will at least be halfway to my goal. How I will travel north from there is a mystery. I used to like mysteries. Right now I'm grumpy and irritable and all I want is for something to go my way.

From Wellington, maybe the train is accessible? If not, then there may be a bus. It's even possible that one of those full airplane seats to Taupo will turn up empty and I can fly standby.

Once I've booked the flight to Wellington I call the number of the Air New Zealand flight attendant I met in Brisbane, hoping she'll invite me to go fishing on their boat. Instead, her father answers and says his daughter and son-in-law have gone north to Karikari and they won't be back for a week. That sinks my fishing hopes.

On this final night in Christchurch I treat myself to a nice dinner … and hope I don't get food poisoning.

Lake Rotorua

THE MINUTE I BOARD THE PLANE TO WELLINGTON MY MOOD improves. We fly north, and below I can see the tops of the spectacular Southern Alps, but the lower altitudes are buried in a shroud of clouds. If I were on a train I would be seeing nothing but fog and rain.

In *Windy Wellington*, as it is affectionately called by locals, a modest gale is sheeting rain across the tarmac. It isn't cold, just unpleasant.

The Taupo plane has already left, but I find an open seat on the plane to Lake Rotorua that leaves in three hours. Taupo and Rotorua are only an hour's drive apart.

I wander over to the express restaurant and eye the New Zealand cuisine. A fatty pork roast, a larded beef roast, fried potatoes and, almost as an afterthought, over-cooked peas and carrots. Six-fifty in New Zealand dollars (roughly $4 US) buys a plate as full as what I'm accustomed to for Thanksgiving dinner back home. And this food is easily as rich in cholesterol as Aunt Melba's butterery milk gravy. I place an order.

"You want cracklin'?" the chunky teenage girl behind the steam table asks as she cuts generous slabs of pork and beef and slides them onto my plate. She points at a shake pile of glistening golden-brown gelatinous skin.

"Uh, no thanks."

New Zealand has one of the highest cardiovascular disease rates in the world. I pointed this out to a New Zealand teenager, who readily agreed the average diet was unhealthy. "But I couldn't go without my meat," she concluded with happy resignation.

The plane to Rotorua is a Saab twin turbo-prop. It jounces up through mashed-potato clouds and levels off to cruise through the heavenly whiteness. Half the way there, we break into sunlight, weaving between mountains of cumulus and catching glimpses of rolling green forest below.

Large jets always feel like cattle cars to me. But small planes are like carnival rides. Our flight is a bumpy one and I keep my seat belt tight. At one point, my hot tea tries to climb out of the styrofoam cup. I sip it down as quickly as I can and then decline a refill when our stewardess catwalks the aisle with a fresh pot.

The strip at Rotorua stretches a meager 4,000 feet along the lakeshore. We descend beneath the anvil cumuli, banking tightly to the left, falling fast toward the slate-blue waves. The plane abruptly levels, the wheels scorch onto the asphalt, and we use the entire runway to stop.

The terminal is straight out of a Bogart movie, with a quaint peaked shake roof, weathered board siding, and Maori woodcarvings framing the front. It reminds me of a hunting lodge in Wisconsin or Canada.

A young fellow strolls out from the terminal and chocks the plane's wheels. Our twin-turbine beast now sits on the cracked tarmac alongside three tail-draggers and a biplane. There is no commotion outside; there are no anxious relatives peering from terminal windows or running to welcome loved ones. The town is on the far side of the lake, perhaps ten miles away. I begin to wonder if cabs ever bother to come here. I see none in the parking lot or along the road.

The stewardess waits to see that I make it safely onto the modified forklift jockeying for position at the cabin doorway. Her name, Yvette, is in black letters on a golden lapel badge.

"How are you getting into town Yvette?"

"A shuttle takes us."

"Think I could tag along?"

"I'll ask." She walks up the narrow aisle, talks with the pilot, then comes back and flashes me a smile. "Sure," she says.

The shuttle turns out to be a large Ford van. On the way into town I start talking about my trip, my writing, and my search for fly-fishing. The driver keeps glancing at me in the mirror. I'm venting my frustration about Christchurch.

"Yeah, those southerners," he confirms, "are not as friendly as we are."

"Why don't you ask Kevin about your fishing?" Yvette points at the driver, then to the rack of tourist brochures on the divider panel. I see the pamphlet titled: *Rotorua Trout Fishing.* On the cover is a girl holding a six-pound rainbow. The legend says: *Ask about his 'No Fish, No Pay' Policy.* It lists Kevin and Lynne Coutts as owners.

The driver chuckles good-naturedly. "I'll get you some good fishing," he says. "I've also got a friend who has a stream on his property. His son caught a thirteen-pounder there last week."

"Great!"

"Where are you staying? I'll give you a call."

I confer briefly with Yvette about the local hotels. The crew's hotel sounds fine, so I tell Kevin he can contact me there.

LIKE EVERYWHERE ELSE I'VE BEEN IN AUSTRALIA AND NEW Zealand this year, the 227-room Millennium Hotel is disconcertingly empty. The Asian currency crisis has crushed tourism. It's good for me: my exchange rate is a wonderfully low fifty-six cents, and rooms are plentiful. My hotel is Korean-owned, and it depends upon Korean tourists.

Practically none of them are traveling; they are waiting to see if their country will go bankrupt. If you are a Korean businessman, no matter how wealthy or respected you may be, flying off to New Zealand wouldn't just be imprudent, it would be arrogant. In the bar the first night there are five people. I remember my experience on the *Coast Starlight*, with the newspaper headline about the Dow's seven percent plunge. *Don't sweat it,* I tell myself. *Things will work out. They always do.*

January 8

Huge Trout

Lynne Coutts picks me up at 1:30 PM the next day. We drive for fifteen minutes, turn down a dead-end street and then down a gravel drive. We park behind two acres of lawn, bordered in front by the lake and on one side by a stream that meanders through brush and trees.

Dennis and Robyn Ward are the owners. He is presently up in the mountains guiding a fishing party. But Simon, their fourteen-year-old son, has volunteered to fill his dad's shoes for the afternoon.

Simon is at the moment of our arrival standing waist-deep in the lake, wearing black rubber waders that are suspended up to his armpits, casting for one of the giant browns schooled up at the stream's mouth. While we wait for him to come in, Robyn serves coffee and homemade fruit cake, then gives me a tour of the guest cottage: two bedrooms, a full kitchen, a living room facing the lake. The price includes trout stream access. Robin asks my opinion about where a ramp could be built. I describe where I would put it and give her a few design suggestions

Simon returns empty-handed. "The browns just aren't biting out on the lake today," he says with patient acceptance.

He is a slim boy with a leader's energy and a quiet demeanor. The kind of kid you hope to find to mow your lawn. The kind of kid you want your daughter to date. Genuine. Sincere. He reminds me of the movie, *A River Runs Through It.*

Before we get started, Simon asks if he can show me the fish he caught last week.

"You bet!" It's not every day you get to see a wild brown trout topping thirteen pounds. And I remember the thrill I had as a boy his age showing off a good catch.

He retrieves it from the freezer, where it awaits taxidermy, cradling the massive fish in his arms. "I caught it with a five-pound tippet, and it took an hour to land," he says proudly, holding it out so I can stroke its rainbow-hued scales. He then carefully rewraps it in plastic and returns it to the freezer.

We walk to the stream. Except for a deep channel tight against the far bank, where the water eddies to form two deep holes, the stream runs only a few inches deep. It's about twenty-five feet across. The banks are stabilized by grass and brush and bermed to keep it from meandering to a new course. The water is clear, the bottom pebbly. Everything seems perfect for trout.

I find a more-or-less level spot along the bank and as I begin to make my first cast I manage a fairly good looping action for a guy who's been out of practice for thirty years. Even so, I'm not quite able to flick the fly into the upstream hole. A light wind is blowing downstream and my line refuses to carry. My efforts continue for several stubborn minutes before Simon finally speaks up.

"I could cast for you," he says, quietly. He has by this time twice had to untangle my fly from a nearby tree.

"I'll try a little longer," I insist, determined to show the boy I can make the line do what I need in order to catch a fish. But on the next cast I again hang up in the tree behind us. Simon, unperturbed, works it loose.

On my next cast the fly goes straight back into the branches. "Damn," I mumble.

As soon as he has pulled it free, I relent. "Maybe it would be better if you did the casting."

Simon takes the rod, wades two yards out into the passive current. Facing downstream he begins to throw the line back and forth in great perfect loops. After he's established an easy rhythm he plops the fly precisely at the top of the upper hole on the backstroke. He gingerly sloshes over to where I'm perched on the bank and hands me the rod, making me feel like a visiting dignitary.

I let the line drift with the current, pulling slightly to keep the fly over the hole and away from the thick mat of grass at the water's edge. I get no strike, so I hand the rod back to Simon.

Again, he wades out, establishes a casting pattern resembling an infinity sign, and plants the fly precisely where he put it the last time. His movement is magnificent and practically on a level with ballet. He hands me the rod without a moment of hesitation. There's no hint that he wishes to fish out the cast. His job has been done perfectly. He's satisfied.

We do this for twenty minutes without any luck. Simon points downstream near where the mouth opens into the lake. "There's another hole down there."

"Let's try it." I doubt it will be any better. I've seen no fish. It's the middle of the afternoon; the sun is hot, and so am I, even though I'm wearing a hat, sunglasses, and SPF 30 sun block. But how can I give up when Simon is so calm, so persistent, so willing to help?

The second hole is equally unproductive. Simon doesn't seem perturbed. His serenity is contagious. If the kid can have this much patience, so can I. My attitude improves, but the fishing doesn't. After an hour, we agree the effort is futile, break the pole down, and head back over the bank.

Kevin Coutts has arrived and is sipping iced tea with Robyn on a bench in the shade of a tree.

"Do you want to try going out in the boat?" he asks.

It seems late to be headed out on the lake. Small waves are kicking up and the breeze that has arisen is constant.

"What do you think?"

"Let's give it a try,"

"You're the pro." I wish he'd said no. I have this vision of three hours in a rocking boat on a bright, windy, fishless day. But I remember Simon's patience and know I am learning a lesson even if I never so much as see the silvery flash of a trout beneath the water's surface.

Kevin loads me into his truck. "I've got a friend with his own boat ramp," he says. "It's not far."

Where I come from, it's doctors, bankers and dentists who own waterfront homes. In New Zealand, it seems there's plenty of lake to go around. Fishing guides can live beside their source of income.

Kevin's friend, Clark Gregor, and his son, John, have a guide service based out of Clark's lakefront house. We pull into the long driveway and find Clark waiting, excited. "Come on," he says. "Let me show you my rental unit before we get out on the boat."

He's *gone wheelchair* with the floor plan of his rental room. The apartment is roomy and easy to negotiate. Even the modern ceramic four-burner cook top has space to pull my chair underneath. He's like a kid showing off. "What do you think?" he asks, leading the way into the bathroom where there are grab bars, a pull-under sink, and toilet rails.

"This is really nice." Which brings a satisfied smile from Clark.

Finally, he leads us out back to the lake. And now I discover just how far Clark has gone to make his business accessible for wheelchairs. His boat, a twenty-six-footer with twin ninety horsepower Yamahas, has a thirty-inch-wide gate between the outboards. An aluminum gangplank extends from the stern to the concrete boat ramp.

Clark proudly struts along the dock as I roll straight onto the boat. I turn to Clark, who stands, grinning widely. "This is amazing!" I say, stunned by how brilliant the set-up is.

"I had it built special."

Kevin pulls the ramp onto the shore and he and Clark cast off. I wheel around the boat and make an inspection. This is made easy by double glass doors which accordion open between the back deck and the fully enclosed cabin. Most boats this size have just one narrow door and it is never wide enough for a wheelchair. I've never seen this degree of accessibility. I want one.

I no longer care whether we catch anything. Just being on a boat built for wheelchairs is a pleasure.

"We'll fish off that point over there," Clark says, pointing far down the shoreline. "There's a weed bank where I've been having good success."

In a few minutes Clark kills one engine and throttles the other back to trolling speed. Kevin and Clark take three rods, each with a spinner and a fly. No live bait is allowed in the lake and I'm skeptical about catching fish. We'll troll at two meters, relying on color and flash to attract the trout.

The wind that vexed my fly-casting is still around, ruffling the water and making it impossible to see below the surface. But the boat has radar, a green screen filled with squiggly red and yellow lines. Clark is showing me how to read it when a fish blip appears.

"There's one," Kevin says, as a red cartoon fish creeps across the screen.

I turn to watch the poles. Nothing happens. I look back. The caricature has disappeared.

Minutes pass. Kevin and Clark sit inside the cabin, talking about weather and politics. I watch the radar, then the poles, then the radar, then the poles. Nothing. I'm anxious, and growing disappointed. But I continue to concentrate. I don't want to miss a nibble; I'm ready to rush to a pole that dips, no matter how slightly. And then something occurs to me. We're fishing for trophy trout with featherweight equipment. I turn to Clark, who is nonchalantly stuffing his pipe with tobacco.

"We're going to know if a fish hits, aren't we?"

"Oh yeah," Clark says, his voice tinged with a Scottish lilt. "We'll know."

I take one last longing look at the rods. It's been half an hour. I think of all the writing I've done since the Reef, and how I've bragged of my luck. Well … humility comes when you least expect it. Even if catching fish isn't in the cards, I can still collect some information and share a pleasant summer afternoon with two fine fellows. I join the two men inside the cabin.

"Are these hatchery trout?"

"Not in Rotorua," Kevin says defensively. "They're all wild. But some other lakes have hatchery stock."

"It's the wild trout people come here for," Clark adds brightly.

Just two trout species populate the lakes and streams of New Zealand: Rainbow and Brown. They have thrived since being introduced decades ago. To protect the fishery, New Zealand bans commercial trout fishing. It even bans farmed fish. You cannot buy a trout in New Zealand. In fact, buying a trout in New Zealand is a crime. A recreational license is the only opportunity to come into possession of a trout. Clark explains why.

"If you could buy trout, it would encourage poachers. A cook might have someone catch a wild one and pretend it was farm-raised, because the wild ones taste better. If you can't buy a trout, it guarantees that only sport fishermen will catch them."

That makes a lot of sense. And because of this regulation, New Zealand has perhaps the best trout sport fishery in the world. Kevin says restaurants caught serving unregistered trout are fined $5,000. But any angler with a license can take a wild trout they've caught into practically any restaurant and they will cook it for you in the style of cuisine you want.

Now, if I could just catch one. Or at least get a strike. But another brief look at the poles, gently bowed by the boat's two mph speed, tells me this may not be the day.

"You want coffee?" Kevin asks calmly, sensing my frustration.

"Sure." He pours me a mug. I've taken no more than three sips when the reel on the left pole goes *Zzzzzzzzzzzzzzzzzzzzzzzzzzzzzzzzzzzzzzzzzzzzzzz!*

"There we are," says Kevin, abandoning his cup and dashing to retrieve the rod. Clark joins him. Kevin hands me the bent rod. The energy of the fish is enormous. They quickly reel in the two other lines and step back.

I'm anxious to get my fish into the boat. I lower the pole, cranking furiously.

"Keep your tip up!" Clark hollers. "And let him run if he wants to!"

My ears burn. Clark had earlier instructed me to keep the pole up, saying half-jokingly that he has a stick to rap the knuckles of fishermen who refuse to follow his directions. I never saw this stick. But Clark insisted, with a headmaster's enthusiasm, that it is stowed somewhere aboard.

In five minutes I have managed to guide my fish to the back of the boat and Kevin scoops it up with the net. It is a beautiful rainbow weighing four pounds, silver with a red blush striping each side.

"Nice one," Kevin says, removing the hook.

We let the lines back out and return to our coffees. I'd be satisfied at this point. But the next trout hits in three minutes.

In the next hour I reel in seven rainbow trout. One was only fifteen inches and no more than a pound and half, a certain keeper back where I come from, but a veritable minnow here so I threw it back. Of the six I've kept, my largest weighs nearly six pounds. And best of all I didn't lose a single fish, despite Clark having to remind me three times to, "Keep that tip up!"

THE NEXT DAY I MEET SIMON'S FATHER, WHO SPECIALIZES IN up-country fly-fishing.

"I know a couple of streams that would work for you," Dennis says with a thoughtful gleam in his eyes. "But we'd have to go in by helicopter." He seems fascinated by the challenge. So am I, but it can't be this trip. Tomorrow, I catch the train to Auckland.

A storm blows in after dark. The gale shreds branches from the trees and the yellow halos of the street lamps outside my hotel room are shrouded by torrential rain. Beneath thick blankets on a comfortable mattress I sleep soundly and dream of fishing for wild rainbows in the crystalline pools of high mountain streams.

JANUARY 9

The Geyserland Express

THE INTERNATIONAL NEWS ON THE DAY I LEAVE ROTORUA IS NOT
good. The Asian currency crisis has deepened. I'm headed toward
Singapore and Thailand at the end of next month. The exchange rate will
make for bargains. But will I be safe? Already, there is talk of revolt in
Indonesia. Papua New Guinea is troubled by civil war. Thailand's Crown
Prince is a wanted man. Students in Kuala Lumpur are unhappy with
president Soeharto. Hard times mean hard rules.

I finish breakfast at the hotel restaurant, put the newspaper down,
and decide to concentrate on today and let the future take care of itself.
There will be plenty of time for worry when—and *if*—it becomes necessary.

I'm taking the *Geyserland Express* out of Taupo. Five rounded aluminum cars, vaguely reminiscent of Airstream trailers, glint in the morning
sun alongside the small station house. The retro-fifties feel is emphasized
inside the coaches by Venetian blinds, bright colors, and sheepskin seat
covers. Everything from the carpet to the door handles is comfortably
worn.

I'm two-man-lifted down the narrow aisle. The wheelchair is stowed
with the baggage. For the four-hour trip to Auckland I'm willing to make
this concession.

The car is full of locals, most of them headed just a few stops up the line to where the busses don't go. In front of me, a heavy Maori woman tries to hold three young children in check, but eventually gives up. They roam the car, exploring every nook and cranny with mischievous eyes. When the train starts, they settle in seats of their own choosing. A boy of six or seven perches across the aisle, throwing me curious glances but refusing to talk to me. Once the train has cleared the town of Rotorua the mother opens a picnic basket of sandwiches and fruit and all three kids scamper back to her.

The narrow-gauge cars ramble along at a leisurely pace to squeaking and squealing of loose steel every time the tracks bend which is practically all the time. After shuffling through the low hills north of Rotorua we enter a broad valley reminiscent of the Salinas in California. The tracks straighten and we gallivant along at fifty miles an hour.

This part of New Zealand is struggling with a drought that has gone on for several years. All along our route I spot lean cattle, a few dirty sheep, dark green corn rows, and fields of squash, cucumber and fresh-mown alfalfa. Where the land is not irrigated, the land suffers. Drought has vanquished the wild emerald-green vegetation and replaced it with a beige underskirt of dry weeds and dead or dying bushes and trees.

I feel as though I'm climbing up from the depths of an emotional well. Christchurch was the bottom. Trout fishing at Rotorua helped a lot. There's still a distance to go, and this feeling is heightened by the bleak towns we now pass through, picking up and dropping off a few passengers at each stop.

Mattamatta barely has a main street. Hamilton, which the conductor announces is New Zealand's eighth largest city, is like stepping into 1963: modest houses with green and red patched metal roofs streaked with rust. Congregations of idle farm equipment. A golf course with exhausted yellow edges and scabbed fairways.

These small rural towns all seem to begin and end with gravel pits, compacted car bodies, sack-piled cement, lumber yards, rows of empty barrels, silos and barns. Their vitality has been leached away, and not just by the drought.

When the European Common Market countries pooled together a few years back and agreed to buy from each other rather than overseas, New Zealand lost a huge market.

The train pulls into Auckland late in the afternoon. The sky is mostly clear, the temperature barely into the seventies. I have no trouble getting a cab. Despite it being a weekday, there's little traffic.

I've been anticipating Auckland for one reason: the Whitbread round-the-world yacht race has just arrived. Every four years the maxi-yachts, with exotic, computer-designed hulls and Kevlar sails, circle the earth. Auckland is a stop this year.

I check into a hotel, then walk two blocks to where the sailboats are moored. It's late afternoon and young people fill the quay's bars and restaurants, drinking, partying, flirting. I join the curious on the pier, eyeing the multi-million-dollar boats. But the viewing is anticlimactic. Without full sails blowing them along at twenty knots, they're just colored hulls, bare masts and wire rigging. Every hatch is battened; the wheels and instrument panels are covered.

The evening chill forces me to make a concession to the weather. A booth is selling race merchandise at reasonable prices. I'm freezing. I buy a jacket with the race logo on it and then wander around for an hour, crowd watching, before heading back to the hotel.

The next morning two young men, one the grandson of Barbara Doyle, owner of the Brian Boru hotel in the town of Thames on the Coromandel Peninsula, pick me up. As we make the two-hour drive east, I'm already considering cutting short the week I've booked at the Brian

Boru. My poor chemistry with New Zealand has returned like the end of a flu. I struggle not to be cranky.

The Brian Boru is free to me because Barbara has agreed to sponsor my stay. She's a bullet of a woman in her sixties, perpetually charged with steamroller optimism. We met on my first trip here in 1990 and discovered a mutual respect for tackling tough odds.

She tries to perk me up by offering a trip to the far side of the Coromandel when she visits her restaurant the day after tomorrow. It's a nice offer, but I doubt it will help my mood. Hours of rural country road driving would drive me nuts.

By the time I crawl into bed, I'm sure I need to move on quickly. Out of respect for Barbara and her enthusiasm for my project, I decide to give it a day or two.

The following morning at breakfast, Barbara announces she is going into Auckland to pick up her sister, who is flying in from South Africa. On impulse, I ask if I can come and try to catch a flight to Melbourne. I was dreading the bus trip; this is a perfect opportunity to go direct to the airport. I won't have the hassle of bus transfers. Barbara is disappointed.

"Is everything okay?"

"I'm sorry Barbara. I'm just … well, I'm just antsy. And I'm bored. It's not you. I need to go where there's something to write about. I need to get moving."

Barbara ponders this quietly. She finally nods in agreement.

"Can you be ready in fifteen minutes?"

"Sure."

In a hurry, I discover I can't cram everything into my bags. It's the new coat! I refuse to throw it away. I want it as a souvenir. Rather than risk busting a seam in my canvas bag or my backpack, I dump the Spanish and Italian cassettes and language books, the mini-cassette player, two shirts and a bottle of shampoo. In fifteen minutes I'm at the van. Three hours later I'm in the air, headed back to Australia.

JANUARY 11

The Penthouse

I ARRIVE IN MELBOURNE A WEEK AHEAD OF SCHEDULE. THE ROOM I intend to rent in a private home may not be open yet. It's 7 PM, so I decide not to call.

I've been talking to a group of five kids I met on the plane. I ask if anyone knows of a cheap motel. One girl says, "Sure!" We pile into a cab, and ten minutes later pull up in front of the Penthouse Motel, a rather seedy looking establishment that I'm not too excited about. *It's for one night*, I remind myself.

The girl dashes in.

"They've got a room," she says when she trots back out. The cabby unloads my wheelchair and bags. They drive off.

Inside, a tired, overweight woman pushes a loud upright vacuum on the worn carpet. There's no evidence of air conditioning. A greasy-spoon cafe opens off the lobby. A cardboard sign thumb-tacked to a board advertises *Live Music*, with a picture of four longhaired men with sullen faces and tattoos. The aromas of stale beer and cigarettes pervade the lobby. *Great choice*, I think, depressed at the prospect, but too proud to ask for another cab.

At the dark brown Formica counter a man in a brown shirt gives me a bored, "Hello."

"You have a room for wheelchairs?"

"Yes. How long?"

"Just for tonight."

He quotes a reasonable rate and says, "I'll need a card imprint."

I hand over my Visa card, the one I carry which has a low limit. My *safe* card. The one I use in uncertain situations. He runs it and then picks a key from the board and comes around the counter and leads me down the dimly lit hallway.

Behind a heavy door sheathed with metal, my room smells worse than the lobby, and my wheelchair barely fits between the bed and the wall. There's a tub with no bench, no chair, no grab bars. Just what do they think *wheelchair accessible* means? That you can actually get a wheelchair inside the room? But I take the key and I thank the clerk. He closes the door and I see it has two locks, plus a lock-bar. A placard warns to keep the door locked at *all* times. I remember the photo of the tattooed band and imagine their clientele is just a little tougher.

I open my suitcase and backpack and pull out my dirty clothes. I'm wearing my last clean shirt. I've worn the same pair of pants for three days. Up the hall I find the laundry room. After my clothes are clean and folded, I call Gilda.

"Hi," she says. "Are you in New Zealand?"

"No, I'm in Melbourne. In a hotel near the airport."

"I thought you were supposed to get here next Sunday."

"I was. I'm a week ahead of schedule. Is it possible to start renting your room tomorrow?" *Please,* I pray. *Please not more than one night in the Penthouse.*

A pause.

"Sure. You can come tomorrow if you want."

The next morning I roll to the train stop, a distance of about four blocks. The train service to Melbourne is great and it reaches practically every neighborhood for miles outside of the city proper. It's 9 AM, but the sun is already fierce. The shelter sits at the edge of a weedy lot and is no more than a roof with three walls, the front open to the tracks. I sit inside with a middle-aged woman, a kid holding a skateboard, and a skinny old man who chain-smokes. They all avoid eye contact with me and with each other.

The ubiquitous Aussie flies have apparently had a little meeting and chosen me as today's primary target. I swat and swipe, and twice try to crush one on my knee, but when the train arrives I've neither killed nor driven them off.

There's an Australian joke: How do Australians salute? By waiving a hand in front of the facen to shoo away the flies. Okay, it's physical humor that doesn't translate too well onto the page. So you'll just have to use your imagination!

I board the train, hopeful that the flies will stay out of the car. Someone has pulled down the windows because there's no air-conditioning. One pesky fly follows me in and vanishes only after we're several minutes down the track.

A Jewish Home

STAYING IN A KOSHER JEWISH HOME is an interesting twist for someone raised a Methodist. When I was searching for a place to stay in Melbourne, Syl told me of her childhood friend, Gilda, who rents her spare room to students. Syl vouched for me, which was sufficient for Gilda. The price agreed upon was cheaper than a hotel, and this is safer than a youth hostel.

I wind up struggling with the do's and don't's of a kosher lifestyle, which seem to mostly involve eating. I'm certain I've mastered the basics until I bring home roasted chicken for lunch. No one's there, so I carefully select my silverware from the meat drawer. I proudly report this to Gilda when she arrives. "The *meat's* not kosher!" she anguishes.

"Oh … ."

She plucks my knife and fork from the sink, handling them as if they were three-day-old anchovies, wraps them in a paper towel, and sets them aside. *Thank God I ate it from the foil package and didn't use a plate!*

She calls her rabbi. He says to bury the utensils for three days; that will be an acceptable method of purification. I manage to miss the backyard ceremony.

I now take nothing for granted. I check and make sure everything I do complies with the kosher code. And because of this, Gilda, her teenaged daughter Talia, and I get along quite well.

JANUARY 19

The Australian Open

BY BIGGEST THRILL IN MELBOURNE IS THE AUSTRALIAN TENNIS Open. On this day I start taking the train into the Tennis Center, about twenty minutes from the house in Caulfield South. A grounds pass costs just $A15, and I luck out and am able to also buy more expensive wheelchair passes for Centre Court, where there is shade and a retractable roof for protection from the occasional thunderstorm which shuts down the outer courts.

On the second day of the tournament there's a Federation Cup *Morning With the Stars* tea at the Hilton Hotel. I'm one of only a few men attending. Most of the hundreds of guests are the *Ladies Who Do Lunch*, Melbourne's female power elite. Evonne Goolagong Cawley, the tennis star of the sixties and early seventies, is the guest speaker.

To get there, I have to walk half a mile from the train station. Having broken a sweat by the time I arrive, I wash in the men's room and change into black pants, a shirt and a tie—my opera clothes. When I come out, Evonne is standing with a small group of women. I join the short reception line, introduce myself, explain my project, and ask if I can have my picture taken with her for the newspaper.

"Of course."

She gracefully moves to my side as I hand my camera to a woman who has agreed to take our picture. I'm scared to put an arm around

Evonne's waist or even to touch her in any way, so I sit with a wooden smile, staring straight at the lens. I feel like I'm twelve years old.

The woman takes our photo and when I check my digital camera the image on the tiny screen reveals an elegant Evonne and a bug-eyed Stan. Later, I have the same experience with Gabrielle Sabatini, except with her, not only do I look overwhelmed, but I also look bald because my short brown hair blends in with the dark background and effectively disappears. But hey ... I've just had my picture taken with two tennis legends.

Livin' large.

FEBRUARY 9

Adelaide

ON THE FLIGHT FROM MELBOURNE TO ADELAIDE I SIT surrounded by members of a professional cricket team. Their coach confides that he has a challenging handful keeping his boys in check. They do seem a bit testosterone-driven. Most teenagers sit more quietly.

"Come and see the game tomorrow," he encourages me.

"Okay, I'll try." But I doubt I will. Cricket matches continue all day. For an American not raised on the game and with no team allegiance, it holds all the charm of pushing a lawn mower. Besides, Adelaide has vicious heat and punishing UV from the southern sun. The *Adelaide Oval* is an outdoor stadium, a frying pan.

Still, I'm tempted. I've nothing specific planned for this stop, other than to catch the fabled *Indian Pacific* train to Perth.

Before we land, I ask a flight attendant where to stay. Acquaintances in Melbourne knew only that Adelaide had beautiful churches and horrible water. Are there are any happening places I should try to stay near?

"Yes, there are places where you can have a good time in Adelaide." She suggests finding a hotel near the casino, which would also put me close to the Art Museum and to the state and municipal buildings.

Once we land, I locate a rack of tourist brochures in the terminal. I pick the Festival Lodge Motel from an economy booklet, and call to make a reservation.

The cab deposits me in front of an older building. The lobby was probably originally designed as a narrow retail space. A brown Formica counter (Was there some special deal on brown Formica in Australia's past?) is wedged along the wall. I ask the clerk if I can see the room first.

We take the elevator to the third floor and he opens the door into a largish room with strange angles and a high ceiling, but plenty of space for the chair. One large casement window provides a generous view of the tarred flat roof that is edged by pigeon-pooped metal flashing. The furniture is Formica and metal and worn fabric. But on the up side my wheels glide easily across the low-pile industrial carpet. A four-inch bathroom step is negotiable; more important, the door is wide and the shower and toilet are easily accessible. With a price of $A60 it's a bargain. Swanky hotels were listed in the airport brochures at $A100-$A300.

Once I've settled in, I hook up my laptop computer. Back in Melbourne a problem developed with the phone and I haven't been able to check my email for two weeks. I click the network dialing icon but nothing happens except for a message that flashes on the screen to confirm no dial tone. I try again. Same result.

I plug the phone back in, dial nine for the desk, and instantly recognize a problem: instead of a digital-type tone, I hear the slow sound of rotary dialing.

"Front desk."

"I'm having trouble getting my computer up onto the Internet."

"I'm not sure you can get on inside the hotel."

"Then I can't stay here. I need to be on the Internet."

"Have you tried putting a nine in front of the number you're dialing?"

That seems too simple.

"No. I'll give it a try. Thanks."

I hang up, try dialing with a nine in front, but still no luck. I go down to the front desk.

"There's an Internet cafe called Ngapartji several blocks up the street," she says. "Maybe they can help you."

"Could you possibly call? I'd hate to walk all that way only to be told 'No.'"

"Sure." When she calls, they say they can't plug my computer into their system.

"I'm going to look around the neighborhood and see if another hotel has tone dialing."

"Okay." She offers a few names.

I spend two hours beating the streets. My search yields nothing but frustration. The hotels I check are either full or have pulse dialing. I return, hot, sweaty and dejected. The clerk now running the desk, a girl of eighteen, asks how my day has gone. I tell her of my difficulties finding Internet access.

"My dad owns an Internet server company," she says positively. "I'll bet he can help. I'll call him, but why don't you bring your computer down first. That way, I can enter whatever changes are needed."

What an angel!

After I bring my laptop down from my room and hand it over, she and her father talk on the phone, and she begins to tap on the keyboard. What seemed like a good idea now seems like a potential disaster. I've no idea whether her changes are to Netscape or Windows, or both. How could I hope to undo them? She hands the computer back. "Try it now."

Back in my room, I get no dial tone. I call downstairs.

"No luck."

"Try putting two commas after the nine."

"Why?"

"Our system is slow. It takes several seconds to get an outside line. A comma tells the system to wait a few seconds. Two commas make it wait twice as long."

I've worked with computers since the early eighties. I thought I knew all the DOS commands. This one is new to me. I try it, and ... it works! The screeching sound of modems shaking hands comes from the speaker. Netscape welcomes me. I switch to Communicator and open the mailbox. There are eight messages.

FEBRUARY 10

A Long Hot Walk

I PLAN TO RIDE THE LEGENDARY *INDIAN PACIFIC* TRAIN TO Perth. It stops for two hours in Adelaide on Tuesdays and Fridays at 3:40 PM. However, my disappointment with the *Sunlander* in Brisbane has made me cautious; I won't spend two days sequestered in a tiny room; not when it costs $A758 for a one-way ticket! So on my second day in Adelaide, I go to check out the train.

A tourist brochure map shows Keswick Station to be on the far side of the city. Adelaide is flat. I count twelve blocks on the simple map, which seems a reasonable distance, and I need the exercise. The skies are clear. A parching breeze drifts in from the Bush, but here in downtown Adelaide it carries in only a few Outback flies.

I leave the hotel at 2 PM, push my chair at a brisk pace down a side street and out onto a major arterial that bisects the city. The sidewalks are filled with business people, mothers with children, an occasional skateboarder, and seniors in formal clothes: men in suits and women in long dresses, proof that the British Empire and Victorian attitudes haven't entirely vanished here.

Tall buildings shade the west side of the street. I bop along, weaving through the masses and slowing only at crossings or bunched groups at bus stops. After two crosswalks I consult my map because I've not yet seen the first named street. I begin to wonder: Just how condensed is this map?

At the next intersection I finally see the first street name on my map and I do the mental math and roughly triple my distance estimate.

I usually enjoy roaming around cities in my chair. It reveals the people, their lives, the bump-and-grind routines that give a city its soul, and there is always the workout of pushing thirty-five extra pounds using just arms. But I'm not enjoying it today. I'm hot, and constantly swatting at flies that don't bite but are annoying. But I refuse to yield. After all, I can catch a cab at any point, right?

I finally reach the city center, a lovely oval park with trees. It's 2:30. I strip off my shirt, trying to ignore the flies that tickle my back and pester my face. I buy an orange soda at a news agency and sit in the shade of one of the park's trees until my sweat has dried.

Off again on what has become somewhat of a mission, and at the next intersection I take a right and go for what seems like forever before I come to the next street named on my map. It's 3:00. The buildings have shrunk to single-story size and my big-building-shadow shade has vanished. I look around but I see no cabs. And the pay phones have also vanished. I'm stuck.

By the time I reach the edge of the city I know this was a mistake. It's 3:30. The train will pull in soon. On the highway I now follow I can't see a train station in the distance, just trees, brush, and one solitary high-rise far off. The highway I'm following borders the city. Four lanes of fast traffic run in opposite channels along a desert-shrubbed median.

A young couple suddenly comes out the unmarked door of an industrial-style building up ahead.

"Excuse me?" I say as I catch up to them. "Is the train station down this road?"

"Yeah," she says. "It's a kilometer, though." There is surprise in her voice. "Are you going to walk?"

"Sure," I tell her and there is that macho pride in my voice which wants to once again prove how invincible I am. I've come this far haven't I? I'm almost there. I feel what seems to be a second wind coming on. "No problem." Really, I'm simply too proud to admit my mistake and ask if I can go in where they just left and use the phone to call a cab.

"Be careful!" she calls out as I push away.

Her estimate of the distance is off. I've gone a mile before I see the station house in the distance. Sweat runnels down my back and drips from my nose. The band of my baseball cap is soaked. I've given up swatting at flies. There are so many and I'm their only available target out here away from the city. Trying to keep them away is a futile effort.

The train has arrived by the time I reach the station. Gleaming corrugated aluminum cars, with proud eagles painted on their sides, stretch along the platform to an engine nearly out of sight. They shimmer in the fierce light.

I reluctantly pull my shirt back on before going inside to find the Trainmaster. A baggage handler directs me to a man who is giving directions to other staff near the main counter.

"Sir?"

"Yes?"

"I've got a ticket to Perth for a week from now. But I need to see if my wheelchair fits. Is there a possibility that I could look at the room?" I hand him my ticket to prove I'm a future passenger and he scans it before handing it back.

"You're in First Class. I don't think you'll have a problem, but let's take a look."

Three cars down, he and the porter lift me up through the main doorway, but the corridor is too narrow for my chair. When I voice this concern they bring out a sturdy-looking aisle chair for disabled passengers, but the porter says the cabin is occupied so they can't cart me down the hallway for an inspection.

"We could raise the blinds and you could look in," he says, hopefully.

"Great."

Back on the platform I peer into the darkened cabin. It looks large enough to turn my chair around in.

"Where's the bathroom?"

"There," the porter says, pointing to an accordion curtain. "It has both a toilet and shower. It's laid out quite well. I'm sure you'll have no trouble. And a porter can take you up to the lounge and dining cars whenever you want." His enthusiasm convinces me.

"I'll see you in a week."

"Good on you!"

I catch a cab back to the hotel.

FEBRUARY 11

Quaint and Friendly

THE WARNINGS ABOUT ADELAIDE'S WATER WERE ACCURATE. EVEN the locals buy bottled water and install filters on their taps to remove the minerals. A friendly local informs me, "It's one of two places in the world where cruise ships refuse to take on water. But if you can stand the taste it's safe enough to drink."

The extreme hardness is a result of where Adelaide is in relation to the source of its water. Most of its water is drawn from the Murray River, which ends its journey here as it flows into the Great Australian Bight, the huge bay formed by the bend of the continent. The Murray's tributaries originate in the low mountains of the Great Dividing Range of the eastern coast, and pass through the desolate center of the continent. By the time it reaches Adelaide, it has meandered through hundreds of miles of Outback, accumulating silt and agricultural run-off and natural minerals from the soil of this ancient continent.

If the land and water are forbidding, the people are the opposite. On my first trip to the public market I stop at a fruit stall to buy a pear for breakfast. A plump woman selling fruit and speaking with a thick Eastern European accent flashes a dumpling smile as she waives off my coins. "No, you take. Is gift!" She turns away before I can protest and begins to arrange apples in a display.

A few minutes later a butcher proudly lets me photograph his meat case filled with kangaroo meat that includes steaks, ground burger, sausage, even jerky. *Skippy* has become a popular alternate meat amongst the health conscious because of its low fat content.

At a cafe, Janet, who is my age, is happy to talk to a Yank. She has friends who are exchange teachers in Seattle and she knows a little about the Pacific Northwest. We sip espresso, talk about Seattle's infamous rain, then about the local drought. When I mention the mineral flavor of Adelaide's water she calls it *interesting*.

I'm captivated by the rural charm of this city of one million. Everyone I meet is helpful. I imagine many who live here have grow up with kitchen linoleum, hankies, tire swings, a local swimming hole, and hard candy at Christmas. My grandmother would have felt right at home. I certainly do.

Later in the week I take a bus tour of the Barossa Valley wine country. All of Australia's major metropolitan areas have their own local vineyards. And without exception, people from each city have told me that their local wines are the best. I'm curious to see if Adelaide's vintages measure up to what I've already tasted in the Hunter Valley.

The medium-sized tour bus twists up a narrow canyon for almost an hour, finally cresting into a rolling country of scorched grass and desiccated gum trees. We pass through two small towns with modest houses that remind me of my home in central Washington State.

As we near the first winery the radio blares out *Rocket Man* by Elton John. I suddenly miss my CD's and wonder what everyone is doing back in Washington. I'm a bit homesick. But there's too much snow back home to want to actually be there now. But I am unsettled. Sometimes, on the road, the smallest event reminds you of the people and the places you love. Passing through a small Australian town has reminded me how much I love a life where people know their neighbors and care about preserving a rural lifestyle. A place where everything is familiar and safe. And that is my hometown of Chelan.

This past week I've been pondering the difficulties I may run into in Singapore and beyond. Well ... obsessing, to be honest. For the first time in my life, I'll be traveling where English isn't the principal language. That's not a big deal for ambulatory travelers. Staying in a room upstairs or having to use a communal shower is not an insurmountable inconvenience for those who can walk, so it matters little if the person you talk to about accommodations puts you in tight quarters or at the top of a stairway. But for someone in a chair, not being able to clearly describe what you need in their language, or to understand someone's answer, is a huge concern.

Or is it? On the *Reef Encounter* I was able to handle very difficult lodging circumstances. But the crew spoke English.

This trip is forcing me to reconsider my previously assumed limitations. I'm learning that sometimes you just have to put your head down and plough forward. So, as I ordered airline tickets and obtained bookings in Singapore and Bangkok this week, I discovered that it has become easier for me to maintain a positive attitude in the face of potential difficulty. I now believe that I can deal with whatever comes up. But I still have trouble getting over the nervousness of traveling in countries where I might not be able to communicate easily.

Here in Adelaide, at the bottom of the world, I'm reinventing myself. I'm learning to put my fears aside for the sake of adventure.

The tour takes up most of the day and although some of the estates we visit are lovely the wines don't measure up to what I've had elsewhere. The reds are too acidic. I'm not a white wine fan so it's hard to appreciate them. Only the dessert wines taste good, particularly the ports. By the end of the day I've barely drunk any wine at all. With a high today of nearly 100 degrees, not imbibing has left me feeling better than most of the others, so I don't mind in the least.

The Indian Pacific

TUESDAY IS A TYPICAL DAY FOR THIS PART OF THE SOUTHERN world. Barely a breeze blows and there is a sense of dust over the horizon. Rain is a distant memory. Summer has gone down to the bone.

I board the *Indian Pacific* for Perth, a line of silvery railcars that stretch for what seems like forever up the tracks pointing towards the west. My cabin is comfortable and easy to maneuver around in and I have the total luxury of a private shower and toilet. The table for my computer is bolted to the wall in front of one of two large windows, which will give me a southern view. Not that there will be much more to see than bush country and desert all the way to the Indian Ocean nearly two thousand miles from here. But I'm still excited about seeing a part of Australia that many Australians haven't seen.

The sun cuts a sharp angle through my windows as I watch my fellow passengers wander around the cement platform in the last minutes before departure, smoking, stretching, talking. For those who began their journey yesterday, in Sydney, this is a precious a chance to go outside. The Indian Pacific makes very few stops during its three-day continental crossing. There simply aren't that many places *to* stop. An announcement over the station's speakers now sends everyone who has gone out onto the ramp scampering back inside.

In a couple of minutes the outside doors close with a hydraulic hiss.

A gentle vibration shudders through the train and my cabin vent begins to whisper cool air from above. I hear the thumps and voices from down the hall of passengers settling in.

The vibration in the metal bones of the train edges up a notch; a porter walks through, pulling doors shut between the cars. A sharp tone comes from my cabin speaker; a man's voice announces the train will leave Keswick Station in one minute. All visitors should now be off.

Outside, the breeze has stilled and the sparse leaves of a small eucalyptus are motionless. Heat shimmers across the platform.

A gentle bump, a small lurch, and we begin to move slowly, smoothly, past people on the platform. A woman and her three-year-old son waive toward the next car. Two men in suits gesture in friendly argument, ignoring we who are departing. Four teenage girls swarm back through the terminal door.

We accelerate past dozens of sidelined rail cars and two locomotives. Five minutes later Keswick is gone, replaced by suburbs of one-story homes built of brick and wood and with economy cars parked in the drives. Next we pass a huge cemetery and it reminds me of how fortunate I am to be alive. The houses thin out and become shabby before farmsteads begin to appear. In less than half an hour Adelaide is behind us, replaced by rolling fields where cattle graze.

The call comes for the first dinner sitting. I'm scheduled for the second sitting, which is just as well. I'm comfortable in my private room with the angled rays of the setting sun striking my chest. I've taken off my shirt. I dislike shirts because my upper body has great sensitivity. Since my accident, that's all my brain has had to work with and I assume my sensory system has adjusted to concentrate upon the skin from the middle of my chest up. I simply feel more comfortable when I'm not wearing clothing on the upper half of my body. Whenever possible, I go shirtless.

Out my window I now see row crops that reach out like corduroy strips toward the gentle hillocks that form the horizon. And where the land is not cultivated it is a soft blend of browns and yellows, weeds and grasses and baked earth, folding like velvet, punctuated by infrequent groves of eucalyptus. Sheep and cattle straggle across this veldt, searching out mouthfuls of the sere grass.

The sun teases the skyline, blazing my cabin with buttery light, and I'm forced to lower the Venetian shade. Soon, the land outside will be a dark mystery. What would stars look like in this vast wilderness? I want to be alone in the desert, looking up, immersed in the Milky Way, with the Southern Cross in all its glory.

The last orange nib of sun winks out below the rolling hills.

At first, it seems there will be no sunset, just a brief candle glow and darkness. But the wispy clouds soon flame yellow and gradually descend into campfire orange. A final thin line of stoplight red quickly cools to blue and black.

I suddenly want to be with people, to hang out in the first-class lounge, to have a glass of wine, to make new friends. I feel the loneliness of the desert night intruding and I pull the shades all the way shut. And finally my call to dinner comes and the porter for my car trundles me up to the lounge car where I transfer back into my wheelchair.

I wind up eating dinner in the lounge car. The diner has narrow aisles and would require two transfers. The lounge, conversely, is open and easy to wheel around in. The porter brings my meal and sets me up at a small round table. The spinach-stuffed chicken and Caesar salad are delicious.

Other passengers drift in. Two Australian couples in their early sixties, taking the trip from Sydney to Perth for the first time, settle in to have a drink and to visit with the strange Yank in the wheelchair. An English couple are pleased about how cheap everything seems. Like my

US dollar, the pound buys roughly twenty-five percent more this year than last. But the newlyweds from New Zealand are on a tight budget. New Zealand continues to fare worse than Australia in the monetary crunch.

When I return to my cabin, the bed is made up. A lot has happened today to make sleep attractive. I climb in but the train's rocking keeps me awake. Unlike the *Coast Starlight*, the rail cars of the *Indian Pacific* are light and their shock absorbers seem to not be as efficient. In relatively flat country, it should be smooth sailing. It's not.

I try to imagine I'm a baby. They sleep so easily, so able to disregard movement, noise and light. And it finally works. Or maybe the tracks have improved? I drift off to sleep. And when I wake up to use the bathroom in the middle of the night the train is moving smoothly.

When I return to sleep I dream that my aunt Melba and my mother are taking me to see grandmother Mable. Somewhere along the way my brother and sister-in-law join us. It's the first time all of these people have been in the same dream. Three of them are no longer alive, but the memories of my aunt, mother and grandmother are vivid.

We walk together down a sloping street, past a row of houses in which my brother and his wife, Melba, Mom, Grandmother, and I live. In the dream, I'm surprised we live on the same street. This has never been so. Why does my dream put us next to each other?

Dreams rarely make sense after I wake up, but I had this dream for a reason. I think my mind is re-ordering my emotions. Pointing out that things have happened in my family, that I need to consider their importance and how they have shaped my life, and that I then need to move on.

The wake-up call comes at 7 AM.

"For first-class passengers holding first-seating tickets, breakfast will be served in the dining car in ten minutes."

I turn my head into the pillow. I want more sleep, but it eludes me. Slivers of light are shafting between the slats of the blinds. The intercom voice says we will notice the change in scenery; that we are now on the Nullarbor Plain and have begun to traverse the longest segment of straight track in the world, 478 kilometers.

I push away the covers and open the blinds. Flatness stretches to the horizon. The Martian orange earth is strewn with rocks and dotted with ankle-high, sage-colored brush that grows no more than knee-high. The funny little shrubs shimmer like punctuation marks upon the vast plain. The plain itself shimmers with heat waves until far away an imaginary lake blues the horizon.

Who discovered this wasteland? I imagine helmeted Englishmen on camels and I wonder if there are bleached skeletons out there, the mortal remains of adventurers who didn't understand the magnitude of this nothingness.

The porter knocks.

"Would you like me to bring you breakfast?"

"Yes. Thank you."

I'll say this about the service on the train. The passengers are always right and the staff work hard to make sure everyone gets what they want. It's refreshing, and I see this as a bright facet of the New Australia. In the Howard government's scheme of things, incentive is provided not by a union-guaranteed paycheck, but by the opportunity for advancement. This train is privately owned. The quality of service far exceeds that on the public trains I've traveled on. Capitalism requires a profit, or the workers go home. The old brand of Australian near-socialism is fading away, especially as the Asians have arrived with a willingness to work themselves ragged to succeed. The old-timers have simply had to adapt.

The train pulls to a stop at noon beside a few forlorn weathered buildings. There is not a wisp of cloud anywhere in the sky. A gust of wind twirls a red dust devil alongside the train and if I were pressed to describe the landscape in three words I would say: Hell has surfaced.

The Service Chief appears in my doorway. He says we'll be here at the town of Cook for a few minutes to take on water. Would I like to get out and see the town? *What town?* I consider wheeling around in the dust and the heat, fighting off the perpetual Outback Aussie flies, thank him for the offer to cart me off the train, and politely decline.

I watch out my windows, from the comfort of my air-conditioned cabin, as several gung-ho passengers de-board and wander aimlessly about on the hardscrabble ground. There is literally no place to walk *to*. The few houses, set in a row 100 yards from the track, are shut up tight. Cook is now a ghost town, although the train brochure says there used to be a sizeable population and even a school. It's hard to picture.

I can see that the flies are fierce here today. Everyone wandering around outside is continuously waiving the Australian salute. Below my window a man points a camcorder out towards Cook. A fly crawls on his left brow and he is trying to ignore it, trying to steadily pan from the houses to the train. He finally stops the camera, takes an angry swat, and walks off.

The only inhabitants tough enough to beat the desert are the snakes, lizards, wedge-tailed eagles, spiders, feral cats, and a zillion rabbits. Earlier today, an educational tape they played over the intercom informed us that the cats and rabbits, both of which were introduced by man in the 20th century, are quickly taking over. The native animal species are disappearing and the rabbits are destroying the fragile plant ecosystem. Even Hell, it seems, has its miscreants!

Just before dinner, I go down to the lounge. As I sip at a rum on the rocks a woman from England, traveling across Australia on her own, tells me she has fallen in love with a man living in Queensland and intends to move there in a few months. A couple from Wales and a couple from Ohio listen patiently. I don't believe she will give up her job and move to Australia. Even though she speaks of love she does not seem convinced this is the right thing for her to do. She seems to be fishing for our thoughts about her intended move, but none of us finds the courage to make an honest comment upon her plans.

We instead move on to a debate over whether the kangaroo fillet described on tonight's menu is worth the risk. And later we discuss tonight's two-hour stop at the gold mining town of Kalgoorlie. Will the one-hour tour be worthwhile?

"There's three kangaroo!" shouts a woman on the other side of the car. Everyone scrambles to look.

Contrary to popular myth, kangaroos rarely come near humans, and almost never near trains. I dash across the aisle, but I'm too late. The kangaroo has already disappeared. It figures. I'm always missing seeing them. So I decide to exact a little revenge and have the kangaroo fillet for dinner and I tell the people I'm with that I have decided to order the filet of kangaroo. A wizened old Australian bloke in his mid-seventies shakes his head. "I wouldn't eat Skippy if they paid me, Mate," he says sagely.

The others are curious when my bacon-wrapped fillets arrive. I cut a piece, dip it in the wild plum sauce, and take a bite. I look up at my skeptical audience and tell them, "It's great. Tender. Not gamey at all. It's like rare sirloin." Despite my endorsement, there are no other takers.

KALGOORLIE, LOCATED A FEW HUNDRED MILES INLAND FROM Perth, is one of the world's richest gold mines. Two square miles of open pit yield a large portion of Australia's gold. This town of 30,000 rises like a miracle from the harsh desert. Many of the hand-hewn-stone buildings have an English Empire look. There is a precious Olympic-sized community pool, and the stained glass church windows rival those of Europe's finest cathedrals. In a kingdom ruled by scorpions and snakes, man has built an oasis.

We slide up to the platform shortly after sunset and outside it is still 90 degrees. We debark in little clutches and wander toward the small station house to shop for souvenirs or to board the tour bus. A group of Aborigines huddles in the shadows by a brick wall, fenced away from the tracks, casually swigging liquor from bottles. Two of them tilt their heads and begin shouting obscenities at the debarking passengers. Within a couple of minutes, police arrive and shoo them away. They grumble, but leave together. My heart aches; they seem so innocent and childlike as they wander off into the darkness, grasping each other for support, posing no threat to anyone.

Of the several Aborigines I've met on this trip all have been kind, entertaining and helpful. For instance, there was the Aboriginal hotel maid in Adelaide who confessed that she admired my courage. I had a great talk with a busker on Sydney's waterfront who was a talented juggler. And, of course, there was tennis great Evonne Goolagong Cawley who took the time to pose for a picture and was one of the most dignified and beautiful people I have ever met.

Aboriginal genetics appear in every walk and station of Australian life. Given the right circumstances, many of them make the transition into the *white man's world*. But in Kalgoorlie? There is so little I know about the cultural clash here, but what I see tells me that in this lonesome place that was until recently only inhabited by Aborigines, inter-racial strife runs very deep.

As our bus returns from the open-pit mine, it briefly detours down

Hay Street. In this dark neighborhood sit three long metal buildings resembling fruit stalls that are lit up only with red Christmas-tree bulbs. Women in black- and red-lace lingerie standing outside on tiny porches now slide back into the dark recesses of their bays, with the exception of two gals who smile wanly and wave as if they are too jaded, or too tired, to care that a bunch of tourists are here to gander at the local hookers. Mining and prostitution are the Jekyll and Hyde of life on this last frontier.

The guide seems to find the prostitutes humorous. "Sometimes, they moon the bus," he tells us.

I am feeling sorry for both the prostitutes and the Aborigines, when I realize something. Probably no member of either group would switch places with me if it meant occupying a wheelchair. I realize that I have been passing judgment upon both of these groups. Is it ever safe to assume that someone else is not happy? Is it ever safe to assume suffering on the part of others? I detest it when "ordinary" people assume I am not happy with my lot in life. And here I am, making assumptions about people about whom I know almost nothing.

WE PULL INTO THE STATION ON THE OUTSKIRTS OF PERTH AT 7 AM the next morning. The air is fresh, the sky clear. I sit next to my bags on the platform, take a deep breath, and say "Goodbye" to the train. I will miss her.

The terminal is a modern structure with a high ceiling and a meandering layout. I find the rack of tourist brochures and leaf through the most promising, folding page corners for hotels that appear inexpensive but not run-down. Everything I mark is on the outskirts of the city; downtown lodging is too costly.

I call the Flag Motor Lodge, and "Yes," they tell me, "we have a room that works for wheelchairs."

"How far away from downtown are you?"

"Six kilometers from the central district. It's only ten minutes by cab."

"How much is a single room?"

"Fifty-eight dollars a night."

"I'll take it."

I don't mind the distance. Being away from the city means being away from distractions. My notes from the train are still only a jumble of impressions. I need to shape them into articles for the *Wenatchee World* and the book. A little forced discipline is sometimes good for the soul. And necessary, if you want to get anything accomplished.

Margaret River

IT TAKES THREE DAYS TO FINISH MY WRITING. DURING THIS TIME I also finally get to use the fancy connector I bought in Hawaii, and am able to hook directly into the Australian-style telephone wall plug. I'm becoming proficient at accessing the Internet. When the manager comes by to check on me, he's surprised to find me sending email. "No one's ever been able to do that here!" He says, standing in amazement as I show him how I accomplished the connection.

I rest for one more day and visit the local casino at night (and win a few dollars!). I am ready by then to leave for Margaret River. It will be my third wine region in Australia, and I consider it a holiday, even though it's a five-hour bus ride to the south.

It's 102 degrees at the bus terminal and diesel exhaust roils from the idling engine of the huge motor coach. Typical of country vehicles in Australia, the front has a heavy wire kangaroo screen. I smile. Skippy couldn't be safer. None will come within miles of the bus with me aboard. I can still count the wild kangaroos I have seen on the fingers of two hands and none of them was up-close.

"How we going get you up there, Mate?" the driver asks.

"No problem," I reply. I've recruited a volunteer from the terminal, and together they easily carry me aboard. As the bus pulls onto the freeway, I feel empowered. This takes a courage I didn't have two years ago, both asking for help, and heading off alone into the unknown aboard a bus.

A story in the morning paper I bought at the news agency in the terminal now dents my happy mood. The angry rhetoric between the US and Iraq continues. Each time I see the public relations battle heat up I wonder how it may affect my plans. Today, while sitting in the terminal, I noticed a small label on my backpack that read, *Made in U.S.A.* I cut it off. I want the look of a backpacker, maybe Canadian, maybe Australian, maybe European. It isn't wise to look American and this is a real sadness.

The bus smooths along at seventy-five miles an hour, stopping in a few towns en route. These towns are set against long pristine beaches, with clean boardwalks, low-rise modern architecture, and ranch style houses overlooking the Indian Ocean. It appears to be an idyllic rural seaside lifestyle.

I'm now just about as far from Seattle as I can get without boarding a boat. From here on, I'm essentially headed home, which is a comforting thought.

Near sunset, we turn off the freeway onto a two-lane country road that winds up through gentle hills that are partly forested with old-growth eucalypts. Occasional vineyards quilt the brown hills. The bus torpedoes along the twisting road for several minutes until we pull into Margaret River. The driver and another passenger help me off and the bus. It leaves a cloud of diesel fumes as it roars off into the night. The street where I sit is dark and deserted. Every business is closed except for a couple of restaurants. I've called ahead and booked a room at the Boodjirup Lodge and they were supposed to send someone to pick me up. Have they forgotten? Finally, a sedan pulls up, and an older man gets out.

"You Mr. Morse?"

"Yes."

"Sorry I'm late. Let's get you up to the Lodge."

The backpacker accommodations turn out to consist of a single room with a double bed, a table, a lamp, shelves for clothing. To my relief there is plenty of room for the chair, so I'm happy.

The bathroom facilities are shared. My hosts find a plastic deck chair to put in the shower. The toilet door is too narrow, but they bring a kitchen chair I can transfer onto and scoot the short distance to the stool. It will work just fine. And for a daily rate of $25, it seems wonderful.

Someone now tells me that *Boodjirup* is an Aboriginal name which means *Place of little ants*. Fortunately, it doesn't live up to its name.

FEBRUARY 23

Margaret River

THE NEXT MORNING I START OUT FOR TOWN IN MY CHAIR, declining the offer of a ride. I need exercise and relish a short, speedy jaunt. From the car last night I remember it being something like a mile. Hard-packed or paved paths are everywhere, making it a paradise for joggers, cyclists and wheelchairs.

I turn left at the end of the street. After what seems like a mile I start to wonder if I remembered the correct direction from last night. It didn't seem this far in the car. I catch up to a woman walking her dog and ask how much further the town is.

"It's back that way," she says, pointing in the direction I've just come from. "This is the way to the river."

"Uh, thanks." It'll be at least two miles now, most of it uphill. I now regret my joyful downhill speeding for the last half-mile.

It's 11 AM when I start back. I break into a sweat and take off my shirt, which is unhealthy with the high UV levels in this part of the world. But I've brought no spare shirt and I don't want to pit it out.

After a pause in the sparse shade of a giant old eucalyptus, I push on, not wanting to catch too much sun and risk a burn. In half an hour I'm finally in town. I find a restroom, wash the stickiness from my arms, chest and face, pull on my shirt and find a coffeehouse. I feel better after a latte and a roll.

The bonus comes when I visit the tourist center and learn the next wine tour leaves in a few minutes. But the bus has no wheelchair lift. The driver is unable to carry me aboard. I'll need something to cushion my rear as I lift myself up the steps. One of the tourist bureau workers rummages around and finds a beach towel in the Lost and Found bin.

"Will this work?"

I fold the towel triple and tape it. Perfect. With the driver steadying my chair, I have no trouble lifting myself aboard the small bus.

There are only four of us and the other three are Englishmen out on holiday. Australians call the English *pomes* (pronounced: *pommies*, as you would say: *mommies*), which is an acronym for *Prisoners of Mother England*. It's not terribly polite and the English are not amused to be called it. I thought the nickname was funny until I learned that Australians call Americans *Septic Tanks*, which according to the Aussies rhymes nicely with *Yanks*. For short, it's *Septics*.

These are two examples of *rhyming slang*, a cultural peculiarity in Australia, and for foreigners it's often hard to decipher. Someone will say *Trouble and Strife* (wife) or *Noah's Ark* (shark). You say "Huh?" and they usually explain, but also give you a *Who let this bloke into the country?* look. The strangest to me is *Dead Horse* which is *tomato sauce* (their sweet form of what Americans call ketchup). It doesn't rhyme at all. Go figure.

These Englishmen are nice guys, as is our driver Nick, and we become a happy little group in search of booze.

We breeze along in our near-empty bus, marveling that back home it's freezing cold, which must make us geniuses or something for being here in the middle of the Australian summer. The more we drink, the more we marvel at our genius. So that by the end of the trip, I doubt Albert Einstein could have held a candle to our intellects.

I buy two expensive bottles of port at the last winery. One, in a triangular bottle, was just too cool looking to pass up. I'll have to ship them home. I couldn't possibly carry them in my luggage for three months, especially after the debacle with the Southern Comfort from Cairns.

We run late. Five wineries, one brewery, and we were never in a hurry to leave at each stop. It's nearing sunset as we approach town. I can't believe my eyes. At the edge of a field stand seven huge kangaroos! "Big reds," Nick confirms nonchalantly.

I'M SO PLEASED WITH THE WINE TOUR THAT I WANT TO TAKE another. The next morning, I wind up in a Jeep Cherokee with an English couple. Our driver is a knowledgeable bloke intent upon educating us foreigners. He says there are fifty-one vineyards in the Margaret River growing region, all planted since the early 1960's when a vacationing American winemaker did a soil survey, then encouraged the planting of wine grapes. Margaret River now boasts twenty-five percent of Australia's medal-winning vintages while producing just five percent of its volume.

At the end of the day we're near the ocean.

"I want to show you my favorite spot," our driver says. He turns off the paved highway onto a dirt road. He parks on a cliff. Before us lies an enormous sweep of slate blue that is the Indian Ocean. The sun is rapidly sinking and out on the horizon the wispy clouds seem to be on fire and the ocean blazes golden where the sun reflects off its surface.

"I've got to get a picture of this!" I say to the driver. "Would you please get my backpack so I can get my camera out?"

"What backpack?" he asks blankly.

"The one I brought with me." There is a sudden metallic taste in my mouth; my palms go moist.

"I didn't see any backpack," he says steadily.

My mind reels. I replay what happened at the tourist bureau. I remember showing the women at the counter my digital camera. Then I took the pack off the back of my chair when I went into the bathroom to wash up and use the toilet. Did I leave it there? How could I have? It's like clothing; I'd have missed it immediately.

I feel numb as he opens the luggage compartment. It's not there.

"I'm sure you didn't have a backpack," he says, closing the hatch.

"Do you remember a dark-green backpack?" I ask the English couple hopefully.

"No," they both say. "We didn't see anything like that."

I'm stunned. We look at each other. No one knows what to say.

"Let's go back to town," the driver finally says. "Maybe someone has turned it in. You can file a police report. Lost things usually get turned in there."

On the way back I'm trying to remember everything that was in the backpack. Two bottles of port, my notebook, emergency wheelchair repair stuff I'd been too lazy to remove from a side-pocket. The pack itself. These are all unimportant. But my digital camera was in that backpack and that truly hurts. Can I find another Kodak DC 120 in this part of the world? Its loss could spell disaster. The images I've taken have made a great difference in my newspaper articles.

We pull to a stop in front of the tourist bureau and the driver dashes in. It's almost closing time for the police department and he wants to take me there too.

"No luck," he says when he returns. "No one turned in a back-pack."

The woman at the desk in the police station is in a hurry to close up so she can post the mail. "I can't do anything today," she says. "You'll have to come back tomorrow and fill out the paperwork."

"Thanks."

The problem with this is that my bus to Perth leaves at 9 AM. Unless I delay my departure, I'll have no chance to file a report.

The driver continues to be sympathetic, but there's a tension developing between us. I wonder if he left the backpack in the street when he loaded my wheelchair and simply doesn't want to confess his blunder. I sense he knows my suspicion.

He takes me to a camping store where I buy a new backpack that is a little less fancy than the one I lost. Back at the Boodjirup, he tells me to call if I need more help; he leaves his card and home phone number.

That night I call the bus company and learn there is a second bus that leaves for Perth at 3 PM the next day. I change my ticket over the phone and then spend a restless night wondering if my camera will be at the police station in the morning.

FEBRUARY 25

A New Camera

THE NEXT MORNING I CHECK OUT OF THE BOODJIRUP AND TAKE a cab into town. The Tourist Bureau has heard nothing about my backpack. I go to the police station and fill out a report, then walk Main Street for an hour talking to merchants and telling them to call the police if anyone shows up with a digital camera for sale.

In the U.S., the DC120 sells for around $700. I consider immediately biting the bullet and calling Camera World in Seattle to have them ship me one. But where would I have them ship it to? I'm in Australia just four more days, and the camera wouldn't arrive in time. I couldn't absolutely count on it getting to Singapore in the week I'll be there. Should I have them send it to Bangkok? But if I do that, I can't take pictures in Singapore. Besides, sending it to a hotel in Thailand seems overly optimistic. I don't want to have to replace it twice. Will a camera store in Perth carry Kodak digitals? Maybe prices are cheaper in Singapore? Or Bangkok? Will *those* countries have Kodak digital camera products? Will they have any digital cameras that I might be able to substitute for the Kodak?

How did I get into this mess? Simple. Something important became a routine. I didn't think about my backpack until the end of the bus tour.

It's a lesson I hammer into my brain over and over: *Never take impor-*

tant things for granted. At least this is a survivable lesson. It will sharpen my awareness, and it may save me from losing my computer ... or my life.

My penance is doing laundry. I have four hours to burn so I find a Laundromat. When I'm done and have all of my clothes neatly folded and re-packed into my new backpack and my suitcase, I call the police. The camera has still not been turned in. I board the bus feeling like a dope.

The driver is a cheerful, talkative Italian who has lived in Australia for the past twenty years. I want to forget about the camera, at least until I reach Perth, so I distract myself by telling the driver about my travels and my writing. He tells me that he's just been home to Rome, and when I mention that my plans include Italy he becomes a font of information.

"Do you like to shop?" he asks.

"Well, yes." Who doesn't? But this isn't a shopping trip.

"You must go to San Marino. No taxes there. Things are cheap."

I rummage in my suitcase for the tiny world atlas I carry. I find San Marino, 100 miles north of Rome and near the Adriatic Sea.

"Yes," he says. "That's it."

"So how's Italy these days?"

"Things are hard. Same problem as in Australia. The government wants to crush the little guy."

"Oh?"

"They're out to bust up the unions." He shakes his head as his voice takes on a hard edge. "No one wants to look out for the little guy these days."

I remember my thoughts about the "new Australia" and the Indian Pacific train and realize here is the other side of that coin.

We talk about there being too many people and too few resources.

Something has to give. I ask him could Australian and Italian workers be more productive? And have guaranteed jobs made them lazy? He agrees… in principle. But his heart lies with the worker, not the boss.

As we near Perth, I start talking to a young Dutch woman who is traveling throughout Australia. She's booked a room at a backpacker motel in the core of the city. "Mind if I tag along with you and see if they have an extra room?"

"Okay." But she's not overly excited. She's a lovely girl and probably gets hit on a lot. Most women are friendly towards a guy in a wheelchair, at first, but as soon as it seems even remotely possible that the guy in the wheelchair might ask them for a date everything swings the opposite direction. How many times have I heard the "boyfriend speech?" Or the "I'm not dating right now speech?" Far too many times. Still, she lets me walk with her to the building and I try not to seem like I'm interested in anything more. In fact, I'm not.

The desk clerk listens to my needs and then says, "I don't think our rooms will work for you, Mate. The doors are too narrow."

"Where should I go?" It's 9 PM. The streets are nearly deserted. I haven't a clue where the better hotels are.

"How much do you want to spend?"

I mull this over. I'm here for just three nights. "I could spend up to one hundred a night," I finally say.

"You want a nice place?"

"Yeah," I say. What the heck! These are my last three days in Australia.

"The Mercure," he says. "It's five-star. They'll have a wheelchair room."

He calls, talks to a clerk, then puts his hand over the mouthpiece. "Is one hundred thirty okay?" He asks.

It is only for three days, and after losing my camera I'm too bummed to want to go searching for a better bargain. "Sure, go ahead," I tell him.

He reserves a room in my name and orders up a cab. The Dutch girl has quietly disappeared.

The Mercure turns out to be posh and suddenly I don't mind the cost. The bathroom is truly accessible, the bed luxurious, and I'm in the heart of downtown. I unpack, connect my computer, and discover I'm back in the land of tone dialing. I log onto Compuserve without a hitch, collect my email, and attempt to send some email messages I've been writing and saving, plus the Margaret River article. My email transmission is immediately rejected. After three tries at sending it through my service provider I try to send it through Compuserve, but I'm unable to figure out how to do this. The pop-up message says I have an invalid address. I can't figure out what that means and eventually I give up. After all I've been through, after all I've learned about the Internet, this seems so unfair.

The next day I find a store which carries Kodak products. They have the DC120. I describe my loss and the clerk is sympathetic. "Back home, I'd pay seven hundred dollars," I tell her.

"Let me check with the manager to see what kind of deal we can offer you," she says. She disappears through a door, returns in three minutes.

"We can give it to you for the equivalent of seven hundred dollars American," she says with a smile.

"Great!" Ask and ye shall receive. The sour taste from my loss begins to disappear.

February 28

Singapore

IT'S 5:30 AM WHEN I LEAVE THE HOTEL TO CATCH MY FLIGHT TO Singapore. The streets are empty. The cabby unconvincingly describes a shortcut to the airport.

"Since I'm about to go off shift I'll take you the quick way."

This makes me nervous. If there's a speedier route why don't all cabs take it? *Wheelchair* seems like a code word for *Easy Target* when people talk weird like this.

We exit the freeway onto a residential boulevard. For several minutes we race down near-empty streets. Only when I see a jet climbing up ahead do I relax. I never find out whether it was a short cut, or whether he was trying to fill every last minute of his shift by taking the scenic route.

The U.S. media have dwelt upon what, to Americans, seems bizarre about Singapore: the Fay boy's caining, chewing gum in public being illegal, littering punishable by imprisonment. It doesn't help when I begin to fill out the entry card near the end of my jet flight and notice the large print declaring that: *SMUGGLING DRUGS IS PUNISHED BY DEATH.*

I get off the plane feeling a bit apprehensive. I immediately notice that security in the Changi Airport terminal is heavy. Police in crisp blue uniforms are everywhere. But most of them are petite young women;

they don't *look* threatening. I smile and they all smile back. Three young women in uniform walk up to me and one introduces herself in near-perfect English.

"May I help you through customs?"

"Thank you."

"Are you visiting us for long?"

"Just seven days."

"I hope you enjoy your stay in Singapore."

"I will, if all the women are as beautiful as the airport officers." This brings smiles; one giggles, raising her hand to hide her mouth and averting her eyes, then looking back coyly. All of my uncertainty melts. *What a schmoozer I am. And I have no shame at all!*

Like a prince, I'm escorted quickly through customs, then to the cabs. Outside it is sweltering, just like in Cairns. Welcome back to life on the Equator.

One of my escorts tells the cabby, in Malay, where to take me. The cabby doesn't say a word during our twenty-minute drive to the hotel and his remoteness makes me uneasy. I remind myself that everyone has said tourists are safe here. Is he Moslem? I sense hostility. I feel exposed in a wheelchair. But we arrive without incident. I pay him and he drives away and I think both of us are relieved.

My hotel is a nondescript concrete building of eight stories, one of many mid-rises lining a busy boulevard. Across the side street is a vast concrete patio with a scattering of plastic chairs and tables fronting several food stalls. I see the words, *Fish Head Soup* on a sign. *Hmmm.*

One of my security escorts back at the airport had asked, curiously, why I was staying in *Little India*. I didn't understand. Now I do. I see Sikh turbans, dark skins, bearded men, women in body wraps and bright scarves. Everyone has full-moon eyes.

Surprisingly, the staff at my hotel are Chinese.

A nimble old porter grabs my bags. He can't weigh more than 100 pounds but he carries the backpack and suitcase as if they were filled with feathers. He leads me eagerly to the elevator, smiling, eyes filled with curiosity and awe, glancing repeatedly at my chair.

The agency I booked through over the Internet assured me the hotel was accessible.

Hardly.

The space between bed and wall is too narrow to avoid scarring the paint with my handrims. The larger problem is the second bed, which blocks off the bathroom. I'll have to get out of my chair and scoot on the floor to reach the toilet and shower and that is impractical. But I have an idea. If the second bed were stood against the wall, it would give me plenty of space.

I look at the old man, who seems ready to do whatever is necessary to make me comfortable. "Can we stand the bed up?"

He shrugs, shakes his head to indicate he doesn't understand. Great. I thought he spoke at least some English.

"Can we move bed?"

Same response.

I try pantomime, pointing at the bathroom door, at the bed, then lifting my hands like a preacher. His smile returns and his eyes widen and he nods vigorously. He moves to the end of the bed and struggles to lift the queen mattress and frame. I'm afraid he'll have a hernia as he grunts and pushes, his slim body willowing, veins popping out on his forehead. The bed teeters upwards and finally settles against the wall with its wooden legs sticking out awkwardly.

He beams a smile. "Goo-bye," he says, bowing as he backs out. I imagine him trying to explain this to the desk staff. I hope he does, because if the maid isn't warned she's going to have the shock of her life trying to figure out how the guest in the wheelchair got that bed frame stood up against the wall!

The bathroom is, essentially, a shower stall with a sink and a toilet. It is tiled all the way up to the tops of the walls. A four-inch threshold keeps water from running out into the bedroom. When the front wheels of my chair are over the threshold the chair immediately wedges against the toilet. It's far enough inside to give me access to the toilet and sink, but just barely.

Electricity must be at a huge premium because the hot water heater is a small metal box bolted half-way up the wall; attached to it is a flexible metal tube ending in a spray wand that reminds me of the set-up in my kitchen sink back home. The switch for turning on the heater is an easy reach but the square water knob isn't. I look around, but there is nothing in the room to use like a stick or a broom or even a toilet cleaner that I might use to turn it with. I try using the shower wand, and at full stretch I can only manage to push it a quarter-turn. *It's just for a week*, I remind myself and decide a cold shower will be okay.

Now, what to sit on to take those cold showers? I can't shower in my wheelchair. And there's no bench or shower chair. Since the porter had trouble with the concept of standing up the bed, I decide that describing a shower chair would be too great a challenge. Suddenly, the solution occurs to me: I can shower while sitting on the toilet.

With the bathroom finally figured out, I now try to get on the Internet. The local number for Compuserve rings; there is the static of computer modems shaking hands, but a message pops up declaring my account can't be verified. The modem disconnects.

"Damn!"

I dial the local help number for Compuserve. No answer. Is it out of date? The room has no phone book. Flustered, I decide to put off trying to gain Internet access and instead begin to write the first part of my article on this city.

Two hours later I'm getting hungry. I go down to the desk to ask about food and to check in the local phone book for the Compuserve number. The woman hands across two massive volumes and at least they are printed in English characters. There is no Compuserve listing in the white or yellow pages. Frustration. Just how do I determine if my number is correct?

Then I remember it's Saturday. The airport cab manager told me Saturdays are slow. Few people work on weekends. "Things shut down here," he said. This ain't Kansas, Toto. I'll wait until Monday and try the number again, hoping the failure to answer my call just means the office staff has gone home for the weekend.

I now venture out of the hotel for the first time, only to discover that Singapore has the biggest fricking curbs I've ever seen. And they have *moats!* Actually they are not moats, they are yard-deep, foot-wide monsoon trenches, infrequently spanned by service ramps.

I work my way down the side street, sometimes using ramps to negotiate short stretches of sidewalk, but mostly risking traffic on the street. Even when I can gain access to the sidewalks, many are blocked by vendors' tables or concrete pillars for awnings or roofs.

It helps that the streets are mostly one-way. With cars coming from one direction it's easier to time my crossings. This is critical, because everyone is in a hurry. A green traffic light seems to start a race, with a barrage of motorcycles popping out in front like a wave of torpedoes. Crosswalks are random and infrequent. Maybe this is a poor district? Maybe along Orchard Road, where embassies and shopping centers are located, there are crosswalks?

I have no idea about what I'll find in the way of restaurants, but what I now see I'm not very excited about. I pass numerous outdoor places where food is being served, usually signed as *Eating Place*. *Fish Head* seems to be the most popular item on the reader board menus.

My appetite isn't encouraged by the beat-up metal chairs and Formica tables sprawled across worn concrete and often flowing out onto the dirty sidewalks. Flies buzz everywhere and small birds forage beneath the tables and on the walkways. The Indians and a few Malays stare at me as if they were seeing a dead relative. Most of these establishments have cliff-like curbs, several steps, or gutter canyons that make it impossible to actually go in if I wanted to. Besides, it's hot and sticky and I crave air conditioning.

If someone tells you that Singapore is one of the cleanest cities in the world, they are *not* referring to these eating places or to the alleys behind them. I walk down two alleys, where trucks are making deliveries, and there is plenty of garbage.

I'm ready to give up and lick my gastronomic wounds back at the hotel, maybe with a candy bar, when I see it. What Australians jokingly call the *American Embassy*. The Golden Arches. Big Mac happiness. In this little corner of expatriated India, the grinning visage of Ronald McDonald beckons.

I wait through two lights, challenging cars that zoom around the corner, and reach the wheelchair-friendly ramp. Then I lose my nerve.

Have I no shame? I'm in Singapore! Surrounded by restaurants where chickens and legs of pork are strung up. Where the sizzle and crackle of stir-fry can be heard. Where the tropical air carries a complex perfume of hot oil, ginger, and saffron. And I'm poised to indulge myself in two all-beef patties? I suddenly resent the relaxed faces of parents inside the clean windows, whose kids are munching handfuls of fries.

And then, only one door down from McDonald's, I see the sign of my salvation: *AIR CONDITIONED FOODCOURT*. Now that's more like it! No American fast food colonialism. But a food court! Visions of the Seattle Center, Coney Island, the Mall of the Americas. Brown trays, clean silverware, straw dispensers and soft ice cream gushing from silver machines.

I walk inside and find the escalators motionless. I search further into the seemingly deserted building, find an elevator. It rises to the second floor, opening onto a hallway fifty yards long, lined with pristine new booths. At the far end a Coke sign glows. Five young policemen sit at two tables drinking sodas. I silently think of them as a gum patrol. They smile at me and I smile back and everything seems right in Kansas.

At the end of the hall is a cafeteria where food stalls line two sides of the room. All but two of the stalls are without signage and shut up with metal curtains. The words *Fish Head* don't appear and I offer a silent prayer of thanks. I choose Chinese over Malaysian and order a bowl of noodles with sliced pork.

"You wan' hot chili?" the wrinkled old woman asks.

"How hot?"

She speaks too little English to explain her idea of what *hot* is. I finally hold my thumb and index finger open a tiny pinch. "Just a little."

She nods.

The only other customer is a wizened Chinese man coaxing beer from a huge bottle into a glass and then taking dignified sips. The police have now left.

She brings my bowl. Thick wheat noodles swim in a clear broth. On top lie pork slices mixed with green onion slivers. A tablespoon of beet-red paste is smudged on three green onion shoots. *Just a pinch?*

As I eat the chili gradually leaches into the broth and by the time

I've consumed most of the broth I can't drink the last of the liquid. My forehead is prickled with sweat. I sip my tea, trying to rinse the flames from my lips and tongue. Despite the sensation that my gums are peeling away from my teeth, I'm happy. This meal cost less than $2 and before the chili began to dissolve it was scrumptious.

I return to my air-conditioned room, flick on the TV, and discover that all programming is in Hindi or Malay. Then the American medical program *ER* comes on in English. I never watch it at home, and finally give up watching it here. I brush my teeth, careful to use bottled water, and go to bed.

It's 10:30 AM the next morning when I finally head back downstairs. As I hand the woman at the desk my key, she says, "We change your room? Maybe better? You look?"

Change my room? After I've triumphed by showering atop the toilet? After I've figured out how to tweak the valve on the heater box with the shower wand? I'm not thrilled. But I'm touched that they care. The porter must have given them an earful. So, what the heck!

"Sure. Okay." At least I should take a look before I get on with my day.

"Not ready now," she says. "Maybe noon. Maybe two."

Great.

"Can I look and see now? I want to go do some things this morning."

She huddles in conference with a maid before returning to the desk. "Okay," she says. "Come now."

We take the elevator to the fourth floor. There are wet towels on the bathroom floor and the bed is stripped. But they were right about it being better. The bathroom is at the front and there's a single queen bed. Even the worktable is accessible.

"Great!" I confirm, smiling.

She beams. The maid beams. I'll bet they can't wait to tell the porter.

Which leaves breakfast. The only option I know of is McDonalds. I again risk three blocks of crazy drivers and massive sidewalks, settling for a sausage patty, scrambled eggs, a potato wedgie, an English muffin and coffee.

I buy a copy of the *Straits Times* Sunday paper and work my way through it and a second cup of coffee, before going back to the hotel around noon. I unpack in my new digs. My first room faced a dull gray office building; the new one fronts a summer-green tree canopy. Re-energized by the improvement in accommodations, I feel ready to tackle the world.

Someone said, "Go see the Raffles Hotel," so I order up a cab. I tell the driver, "Raffles Hotel," and he launches at break-neck speed through narrow streets crowded with cars, three-wheeled vendor carts, pedestrians, bicycles and motorcycles. Why so fast? He is driving a lightweight car that would give little protection in a crash. I want to grip the seat the entire way but I refuse to lose face by showing my fear. I'm amazed we don't crash before reaching Orchard Road, the main thoroughfare, where they still drive crazily but at least there are wider lanes and fewer obstacles.

The Raffles Hotel is a British Empire gem. Two turbaned Indians, with livery straight from a Hope-Crosby road movie, come out to the gravel drive. One anxiously fails to assemble my wheelchair. "Let me," I say repeatedly, and finally he stands back to marvel as I pop the wheels on and casually swing into the chair from the cab. Eagerly, they carry me up the steps to the massive front doors.

It's still the nineteenth century inside. A sweeping Scarlet O'Hara staircase, enough mahogany paneling and railing to build a ship, a Hollywood floral arrangement that is almost a forest, spit-and-polish brass, marble floors, Persian carpets, crystal chandeliers. I half-expect to see Jay Gatsby and Teddy Roosevelt planning a tiger hunt at the long bar.

I wander around like a twelve-year-old, absolutely entranced by the majesty of the place. I spot a couple drinking from glasses that bear the words: *Singapore Sling,* and remember a brochure I read which said that this is the place where they were first concocted. Souvenir glass in hand, he says to her, "Take a picture of me." They're Americans. She gets up with a camera. I move forward.

"Let me take the two of you together."

"Oh, that's nice!" They cozy up, I click twice. Hand the camera back.

"Where you folks from?"

"Ohio. And you?"

"Washington State." I describe my project, and they become instant fans.

"I'll look for your byline," the husband says when I leave. "Good luck!" And the wife adds, "If you're ever in Ohio, look us up!" I think she actually means it.

At a shopping center across the street I buy an inexpensive cassette player, regretting the one I dumped at the Brian Boru. I hope to learn a few basic French words from the tapes I kept, having been repeatedly warned that the French will expect me to take a stab, however grotesquely executed, at speaking their language.

Back out on the street I hail a cab. The cabby is a talker. He points out fancy hotels, including the Intercontinental. "Very expensive," he says as we pass the monolithic building. "What you paying?"

"Sixty."

"That is bargain," he says. "The hotel next to you, two hundred. Hilton three hundred. Better you spend money on other things." We both chuckle.

The ride back to my hotel costs $3.40.

March 2

Embassy Interview

My Monday call to Compuserve goes straight through. The technician, an Australian in Sydney, talks me through the screens and commands. I had the wrong domain listed, whatever a domain is. I hang up with the technician and log on with no problem. Until I try email. *Transfer denied*, it flashes.

I fiddle with the software for two frustrating hours. Nothing works. I call the help number again. "It should work," the tech says. "Maybe it's your server?"

I decide to find an Internet cafe in Singapore and send my server an email explaining the problem. Then I realize the email problem may go both ways. What if I can't receive? There were no messages in the queue when I clicked the receive icon. How would they contact me? So I decide to call. It's big bucks but I see no alternative.

Unfortunately, Washington is fifteen hours behind me, and counting the international date line it's *yesterday* back home, which means it's Sunday and my provider is closed. My window for calling starts at midnight and ends at 8 AM. I have no alternative but to wait.

To fill out the day, I catch a cab to the American Embassy, hoping I can interview someone about how our embassies function. An earlier call gave me the name of an information officer who might be available. Then, in the middle of the city, I see a Starbucks sign.

"Stop there!" I shout, pointing. The cabby drops me in front. I regularly went to the original Starbucks in Seattle's Pike Place Market back in the early eighties. I never expected to see one in Singapore!

First McDonalds, and now Starbucks. This is a strange new colonialism.

I order a grande latte and it tastes just like Seattle.

At the next table sit two women in their late twenties, wearing big diamond rings, Americans by their accents. Sometimes I amaze even myself with my willingness to make an impromptu introduction.

"I'm sorry," I cut into their conversation. "But I'm desperate to talk to Americans. I've been on the road for four months. May I join you?"

"Sure," they say simultaneously. A chair is scooted away and I pull in to their table.

They tell me that their husbands work in Singapore. I tell them about Australia. Both want to vacation there; neither has been before. It feels so good to be with other Americans, even for a few minutes.

I eventually catch a cab to the Embassy. I pictured it as a quaint Louisiana mansion. The women at Starbucks smiled at my naive description. One teased that it would "rise up before me." The other assured me that, "You couldn't possibly miss it."

Still, I am unprepared for the 114,000-square-foot, five-story, granite leviathan, with the seal of the United States of America emblazoned on the front. Neither am I prepared for the security.

I'm admitted past the thick glass doors at the first gate only after the guard carefully scans my passport and determines I'm an American. I thought an American journalist (well, okay, a quasi-journalist) would have no problem taking a digital camera inside. Wrong.

"No electronic devices allowed," the officer says sternly. He pushes a plastic tub across the counter. "In here, please. Your business?"

"I came to interview the Information Officer."

They call the IO's secretary. She says to go to the reception area; he'll call the desk as soon as he's finished a meeting.

One of the guards pushes me up the long ramp. It runs parallel to the front of the building, making it impossible to rush the front door or detonate a bomb near the building. It feels like I'm entering a pyramid.

At the top the guard pushes open an inch-thick glass door that looks like transparent steel. I'm escorted to a small but comfortable lounge area where several Americans are watching CNN. When I ask why they're here, they say they've come to prepare and file their income tax returns.

Shortly, a woman comes out. "Mr. Morse. Mr. Anderson's on the line." She shows me to a phone cubicle and closes the door behind me. He says he'll be down in five minutes. I'm nervous. I thought this would be fun. Now, I feel like I'm intruding.

When I come out, a man jokingly says, "We heard you were a journalist, so we tried to lock you in." Everyone but me laughs.

"I'm just a travel journalist. And I'm pretty new at it." This seems to appease them; they return to watching TV without further comment. I'm surprised by their hostility, then realize I have the same attitude. I'm tired of sensationalism. Journalists cause more problems than lawyers!

Michael H. Anderson turns out to be a nice guy and very professional. He gets me talking about what I'm doing and before I realize it our half hour is up. He gives me some printed material. I need to work on my interviewing skills. But for now, I'm happy it went well, and I'm glad it's over.

I've learned that the embassy in Singapore is anything but small-time. Singapore is the eighth largest trading partner of the U.S. Quite a feat for a country of around three million. It's also the region's banking center, nicknamed the Switzerland of Southeast Asia. This embassy is our diplomatic hub for Malaysia, Thailand, Vietnam, Cambodia, Burma and Laos. The FAA is here. The Department of Agriculture. The IRS. The Foreign Commercial Service and the U.S. Information Service. A veritable microcosm of American government.

Later, I wonder if I would have cold-called Mr. Anderson if I had known how serious the operation is. Probably not. But I'm glad I went. It helped me appreciate the extent of our diplomatic relations.

MARCH 3

Singapore

THE NEXT MORNING I CALL MY INTERNET PROVIDER IN Washington.

"Hello?"

"Hi. It's Stan Morse. I'm in Singapore. I can't get my email to go through."

"Oh. That's because we changed it so you can only send email if you're in our area code."

"Why?"

"We were getting spammed."

"Spammed?"

"Someone was using us to dump junk advertising."

"Oh ... well, how do I send my email?"

"Who are you using to connect now?"

"Compuserve."

"Just enter 'mail.compuserve.com' as your SMTP server."

Typical tekkie advice. What in the world is an SMTP server? I decide not to try for an education. Directions will be so much easier while I've got this guy on the line.

"Can you help me through it?"

"Sure."

He talks me through the screens. This is costing a fortune in long distance. It better solve the problem! Fortunately, it does. After he's hung up, I'm able to send and receive email.

There are certain maxims it is wise to follow: Don't eat fish in the desert. Stay out of dark alleys. Keep your sixteen-year-old son away from the new car. And never order from a menu without prices.

The Bee Hiang Fish Head Steamboat Restaurant sits across the side street from my hotel. It features patio dining from open stalls. I presume the Bee Hiang will be relatively inexpensive, since it's casual and outdoor, so I order what looks appetizing: Shark Fin Soup with Crab Meat, Black Pepper Ostrich, and that old standard, Sweet and Sour Chicken. There are no prices on the menu, just pictures. Five bucks each, right?

Wrong.

When the $47.70 bill is presented my eyes must almost literally bug out because the waitress takes a step back.

"What was the expensive one?" I blurt out. She leaves me to consider the bill, which except for the numbers is written in Chinese. The $20 entree must be the Shark Fin Soup. Thank heavens I didn't order the Birds' Nest Soup!

My remaining days here are filled with little wonders, like the crows that gather their murder in the leafy trees outside my room as they jungle-up each night. At dusk they caw loud enough to drown out the TV, raucously jockeying with each other for a comfortable perch on the crowded branches. Every morning the same ruckus erupts as they scavenge away. There's no need for an alarm clock here; just listen for the birds at sunrise.

My cautions subside. The first day, I wasn't willing to risk rinsing my mouth with tap water. But I gradually accept that the Singaporean government operates a sanitary water system. Life in this city is safe.

I never get used to the humidity or the manic drivers and the congested traffic. But I come to like the Singaporeans. More than once, someone comes running to open a door for me. Strangers repeatedly commend my courage. It would be hard not to like them.

Seven days fly by.

On the way to the airport on the day I leave, the cabby seems to think the white lines dividing the three lanes of traffic are merely suggestions about where cars should travel. He ignores the vehicle's (apparently ornamental) turn signal, changing lanes with no warning to other motorists. Even by Singaporean driving standards he's reckless. I'm scared to look and see how closely we cut people off. I say a prayer and think about the snow back home.

Changi Airport is different when you're outbound. Coming in you are routed directly through. You miss the gym, sauna, Internet cafe, gourmet restaurants, and stores selling everything from cameras to Italian handbags to French perfume to sunglasses to ... well, you name it and Changi has stores selling it.

Most amazing are the outdoor pool and hot tub. I've never swam at an airport. I rent towels and a locker for $6 and go in the men's room to change into my swimsuit.

In most public places, particularly in foreign countries, I'm uncomfortable changing in a public dressing room, or leaving my computer, digital camera, traveler's checks and passport in a locker. In Singapore, it feels safe.

Once I'm in the water, the heat and humidity become enjoyable. I talk to an English couple lounging beside the pool; then to a young Swiss woman in the hot tub. I watch jets landing and taking off. An airport swimming pool. What a concept!

I needed this swim to relieve the stress of going to Bangkok. People in Australia, when they heard I was spending a week there, shook their heads in disbelief. "No need to spend more than a day," one said warily.

A local Starbucks manager, who took quite a shine to me, became suddenly serious when he learned of my next destination. "You be careful. It's hard times in Thailand. People are desperate there."

March 8

Bangkok

Bangkok at midnight. The customs officers, military men with stone expressions, are tense. I'm wondering if something dramatic may happen at any moment. It is such a vast difference from friendly Singapore. Did the Asian economic crisis, which began last year when Thailand floated its currency, create this grimness? Or were they always like this?

The aircraft captain said we would need 650 baht for the cab ride into the city. So when I enter the lobby I look for a currency booth. The only one open has a long line, but there is a currency exchange machine nearby, a *non sequitur* in a society where human labor is cheap. American dollars, Australian dollars, English pounds, French francs, German marks, Japanese yen; you feed in a bill, punch a button, and it spits out the equivalent in Thai baht. It sucks in my $20 American bill and 863 baht shoot into the tray.

Baht in hand, I'm practically accosted by what I will call the *cab pimp*.

"You need cab?" a man in a bright yellow coat, who scurries from across the lobby, demands. "Six hundred fifty baht."

The *cab pimp* shifts nervously, as if he might be expecting flames to erupt from the floor at any second. I peel off a 500 and two 100's and he grabs them, returning a 50 coin and a slip of green paper. "Come over here," the *cab pimp* orders. He takes me a few feet beyond the melee which is erupting at his company's counter, quickly deserts me, and zeroes in on another dazed tourist. I'm too intimidated to be entertained by the carnivalesque frenzy as other passengers are culled out by the *cab pimp* like apples from a bin.

My friends in Adelaide warned me to watch out for *referrals*. Kickbacks are common rewards for Thais who recruit customers for hotels, restaurants, etc. So when the yellow jacketed *cab pimp* comes back and asks, "Where you stay?" and I say, "Tower Inn," and he says, "You pay yet? You have reservation?" I recognize the scam.

"I've paid," I say firmly. It's a lie; but the last thing I want is to be sent to a hotel where accessibility is an unknown.

His face contorts in frustration and he immediately walks away.

I hate this process. Why can't he just get me a cab and settle for that one hustle? This is weakness on my part. I'm in a tough part of the world, made tougher by the recession. I need to be firm, in control, to give the impression that I know the ropes. I need to become bullshit-proof.

I'm finally ushered out into the 90-degree night. For the first time I smell the air: it stinks like a combination of forest fire, burning tires and a stinky oil refinery. A population of fifteen million generates a horrendous amount of pollution, and also being one of the hottest cities in the world doesn't help the situation. I sink into the front seat and buckle up, grateful for the sudden wash of conditioned air that cools the perspiration on my face and arms.

The wiry driver glares tiredly. "Where you stay?" he asks in a clipped sing-song voice.

"Tower Inn."

"Where?" he asks searchingly. Never mind that it has 500 rooms. Never mind that it's in the heart of the city. He's in recruitment mode from the get-go just like the *cab pimp* was. But by now I'm prepared. I pull out the hotel brochure and hand it across.

"Tower Inn," I repeat. He flicks on the dome light. Holding the steering wheel with one hand he fumbles the brochure open. We are now doing 100 km/hour down a nearly empty street.

He studies the brochure, gives a few tight shakes of his head, and his brow crinkles as if it has him greatly perplexed.

"You pay already?"

I want to shout, *Of course I've paid! So take me to the hotel!* But one of the things you live with in a wheelchair is the reality that if you piss someone off, there's nothing to prevent them from stopping the car and shoving you onto the road. So I'm polite.

"Yes, I've paid. Have special wheelchair room."

He returns a blank stare that looks far too practiced. We're playing the game now. He knows I'm tired and that all I really want is to climb into a bed. *Any bed.* If I show weakness, he'll take me to another hotel.

"Special room at Tower Inn," I repeat slowly, pointing at my wheel-chair, which lies disassembled in the back seat. "They have special room."

Without looking at me he gives a brief nod, then glares straight ahead.

We ramp onto a freeway and the speedometer dials up to 130. I offer a silent prayer of thanks for the sparse traffic.

Having paid a set fee of 650 baht, I'm not concerned he'll drive around aimlessly to run up the meter. So when we loop away from the tall downtown buildings I get nervous. I'm with a man who probably has a wife and kids to feed. He's making next to nothing for this half-hour ride. He would expect me to have cash. And there's that fancy, valuable wheelchair in the back seat ....

Stop it! I have to stop thinking this way. I put on my best game face, confident and relaxed.

We finally turn back in the direction of the tall buildings. In a few minutes he exits the freeway onto a deserted downtown street. In four blocks we stop at an intersection. He points up ahead.

"See, there Silom Road." He gives a toothy smile.

Three blocks later he points at a huge neon sign.

"Tower Inn," he proclaims confidently, pulling into a driveway beside the hotel as if he's been here a thousand times. He probably has. And now he's being polite on the off chance that I might give him a tip for suddenly being so courteous. There are two steps and no ramp at the front of the hotel but I say nothing. I'll cope with it.

As soon as my bags are piled on the sidewalk and I've given him a small tip he jumps back into his cab and accelerates back onto the street.

A porter and a security guard lift me up the steps. Inside, there is a brief moment of panic while they search for my reservation, but the girl finally finds my name. No one speaks much English. I realize, from their cautious glances that they rarely get wheelchair travelers. But they are being polite.

I'm handed a key. A security guard joins us at the elevator. Why do we need security at 2 AM? We ride in silence to the fourteenth floor. When the porter opens the door, the room is fine, huge actually, with a king-sized bed; but the bathroom door is too narrow to admit my chair. Even if I could get through, the door itself blocks off the shower. The only solution is to remove the door. No way am I going to get down on the floor and scoot around on my rear for a week to use the bathroom. And no way am I going to go looking for another hotel room in the middle of the night. There is only one practical solution.

I point at the bathroom door. "I can't fit. Need to take door off hinges."

The porter is confused.

"Have to take off hinges," I repeat, holding my hands as wide as the bathroom door, then holding them above my wheels to show my chair is wider by one miserable inch.

Comprehension dawns on his face. "I get building engineer," he says.

Oh great! At 2:00 AM? "No. Just need to pull pins," I insist, suddenly feeling very tired and frustrated. This can be so easy. "Just need screwdriver." There are three pins; we can pull them out. But the porter ignores my plea and immediately heads into the hallway. I look at the security officer, who returns a bland, non-committal look. He speaks no English.

The porter returns in ten minutes with a middle-aged man who carries pliers, a screwdriver and a hammer. They are accompanied by another guard. We are now a five-some.

The engineer puts the blade of the screwdriver to one of the screws and starts to turn.

"No," I say politely, but insistently. "Just need to remove pins." I'm amazed that he apparently intends to remove the hinges from the doorframe. I point to the pins, gesturing as if I were using the screwdriver to loosen them, then show how I would pull them with the pliers. There is no excitement on his face at this revelation. But I'm the customer, so he half-heartedly bangs away with the screwdriver and hammer. The screwdriver repeatedly slips off the pin. After three attempts he shrugs, then patiently removes eleven screws.

The twelfth screw refuses to come out so he hammers the screwdriver under the hinge and pries it away from the jam. It breaks free with a chunk of rot-blackened wood clinging to the screw. The engineer and the porter take the door out into the hall, standing it like a monument against the wall.

I am so glad that the *cab pimp* and the cabbie aren't here to witness this impromptu remodel job, because I'm certain they would tell me of hotels where the doors are plenty wide! With cheaper rates, and closer to important shrines. And no doubt owned by their uncle or cousin.

After my little construction crew and their security escort leave, I fall into bed and sleep until 10 AM.

MY BEST DISCOVERY IN THE PEOPLE I MEET AT THE HOTEL IS AN Englishman in his sixties who came to Bangkok on the spur of the moment with an older male friend, I suspect out of boredom and depression. I meet him at dinner the first night, just before he's ready to visit the Patpong, Bangkok's red-light district three blocks away. He's a jovial man with a greying beard—a slim version of Burl Ives—hell-bent on having a good time. He carries on about the beautiful girls and how, for a few drinks, they become very friendly. I don't ask for specifics.

I've seen bar girls in the hotel, accompanying men who are grossly overweight, in poor health, old. They hang on arms, stroking the shoulder or hair of their newest fella. Asking questions. "You not married? You don't have girlfriend back home?" It's pathetic. The girl hopes he'll fall in love long enough to buy an expensive gift or a few meals, and to slip her some cash. It's more emotional than physical prostitution. And that's sadder. At least with physical prostitution there's a deal, an act, a payment, an ending. But this hopeless coupling continues to drum home what is unapproachable for the girl, long lost by the man.

I know about loneliness. You cannot be in a wheelchair and not feel a degree of isolation. But I also know about love. And anyone who hopes for love would never seek out the Patpong.

As we eat, the Englishman slides his leg out from under the table so it is straight and more comfortable. The pants are split near the bottom; he wears a slipper rather than a shoe. The leg is red and swollen up to mid-calf.

"Scratched it on some sandals I bought up-country," he says matter-of-factly. "I told the doctor I washed it off in the shower and she said I shouldn't have done that. I should have covered it with a plastic bag and not gotten it wet because the water isn't good."

This is frightening. I clipped my toenails today, and I often nick the skin. I also have an infected cuticle on my left pinkie.

After dinner, I return to my room and douse each toenail with iodine, then lance the slightly-swollen tip of my finger with a needle and squeeze out a small amount of brown puss. I then carefully iodize and bandage it.

March 9

Sapphires & Rubies

INTIMIDATED BY THE CITY, I DON'T VENTURE OUT UNTIL THE second day to find a bank where I can change some currency. The sidewalk is filthy, the concrete often broken or uneven. At alleys and intersections the curbs are high and irregular. But the real danger, I discover, is motorcycles. Before I realize what is happening, one zips by me at twenty mph, passing within inches of my right wheel. I was warned to be careful crossing the streets, but nothing was said about this!

On the way back from the bank I stop at a jewelry shop. I've heard about the local sapphires and rubies.

For the next hour I'm their only customer, attended by women who bring a delicate, chilled jasmine tea and patiently let me look at dozens of stones. I'm hooked, but have no idea what they sell for back in the U.S. What is a bargain?

"Take my card," the owner says as I apologize repeatedly for not buying. "Call me if I can come and show you something at your hotel room." She speaks the best English of any local I've met. I feel guilty for having taken her time. Four-carat cabochon sapphires for $250 seem cheap, but I leave empty-handed.

You learn quickly that no one is sincere. So many try to hit on you. They have something to sell. They want to introduce you to someone who has something to sell. Their brother has a discount business. They know a nice girl. The hustle is non-stop. It's like being surrounded by used-car salesmen. And they're good at it.

After being pursued by people selling everything from suits to watches to gems, I get the uneasy feeling of imminent dispossession. Of my money. My computer. My camera. Even my health or my life.

Years ago, I had a glimpse of this feeling when I bought my first house. I went out to get my mail from the box and, when I returned, I found my duplicate key didn't work. I was locked out during winter, momentarily homeless. I called a locksmith from the neighbor's. As he fiddled with my lock I swore to never forget how brutal life can turn in an instant.

Life is brutal for many here in Bangkok. I'll never forget that.

MARCH 10

Sidewalk Odyssey

FRIENDS IN ADELAIDE HAVE GIVEN ME THE NAME OF THEIR tailor and said the custom-made suits are good and come at bargain prices. On the third day, I order a cab and give directions for the Oriental Hotel, near the tailor's shop.

We criss-cross the downtown, rather than go straight to the hotel. I'm certain the cabby is extending the trip to run up the fair a bit, but I don't mind. I'm getting a tour. And a lesson about traffic. We come closer than six inches to dozens of motorcycles and hundreds of cars and busses.

The motorcyclists are all kamikaze. They scrunch like Power Rangers in nylon suits with Darth Vader visors, on bright-colored crotch-rockets which careen through the traffic-choked streets, missing cars by inches, sometimes fractions of an inch, occasionally brushing a fender. If one went down, it would probably take three or four vehicles running him over before traffic begrudgingly ground to a halt. It's jungle rules. And that counts double for pedestrians. People on foot get zero respect. What are you going to do, sue?

The cab finally deposits me outside the Oriental Hotel. I find a veranda overlooking the river, and watch skiffs with motors mounted on gimbals zoom past. The drive shafts come straight from the motor; the propeller is dipped into the water and steered with a swing of the engine. It is as dangerous as everything else seems to be in this city.

A few well-dressed tourists are lunching, no doubt congratulating themselves for staying in a famous landmark. They will return home with tales of how they *Did Bangkok*. But you don't *do* this city unless you walk its streets. You must leave the fringe of tame shops which surround the Oriental and experience the squalor and poverty. And then, all you want to do is turn away, go back to the safety of the hotel, and try to forget that a place like this can exist.

After half an hour I walk to the nearby tailor shop. The woman whose name I was given is gone today. Another helps me. I choose two conservative gray bolts of Merino wool. She calls the Indian tailor, who carefully takes my measurements.

When he's done, she says, "I can bring them to your hotel tomorrow or the next day for the final fitting."

"The day after tomorrow is fine." I knew it would take very little time, but this turn-around is stunning. I've ordered custom suits that took weeks, even months. I'm paying $200 each, and that's with two pair of pants per suit. My Adelaide friends were right: these are a bargain.

I decide to risk it on foot back to the hotel. It's noon. Outside it's hot, humid and smelly, but I'm determined. I figure it to be a mile, straight up Silom Road. I can always stop and catch a cab. And as long as I look for traffic, I should be okay.

Everything goes well for several blocks. I'm hopping the twelve-inch curbs, and finding ways around those which are higher. But I lose concentration for just a moment and hit a cleft in the sidewalk. My front wheels catch, wedge, and suddenly I'm rocked forward, my rear wheels come off the ground, and my weight shifts onto the front bar and wheels. My rear slides forward on the black nylon cushion. My gloved hands slap down on the pavement. I teeter. Then, I carefully inch my rear back onto the cushion, heart hammering. The chair settles back onto all four wheels.

Two European tourists behind me don't so much as pause to see if I need help. And no Thai seems the least interested. If I'd fallen out, I'd have been left to my own devices.

Bangkok will have its defenders. They will say the exotic and the mysterious come together here. That in its crowded streets, a beautiful people work hard against great odds. True. If you are a romantic. But on foot, it's hard to be romantic while choking on the blue smoke boiling up from traffic, eyes tearing, dodging errant cycles, rolling across dog feces and God knows what else caked on the concrete.

If I ever come back to Thailand, it will be to some place like Phukhet, with its white beaches and pristine ocean, and far from Bangkok's survival dramas.

I SEE THE ENGLISHMAN AT DINNER AND TELL HIM OF MY adventure.

"Good going," he says.

"How are things with you?"

"Not good. My friend," he says, "thinks he's in love, and there's nothing I can do or say to change his mind."

"Who is she?"

"Just a hooker, but you could never convince him of that. You know, he's seventy, and she's only forty ... at least she says she's forty. He's already bought her several expensive gifts, jewelry, clothes. And he can't see what's happening. He's dizzy."

"Can't you do anything?"

"What would I do? They're off in the countryside somewhere. We're supposed to fly back to London tomorrow. I don't even know if he'll show up for the flight."

"I'm sorry."

"Well, maybe it's not so bad. At least he's happy. There are worse things, I suppose. But his family isn't going to like it."

"How's your foot?"

He holds it out. It's still red and puffy. I'd be in a panic by now if it were mine; I'd have raced to the airport and caught a plane to get good medical care. But he seems unconcerned. "I'll get it looked at back home," he says. "It's gone down a lot."

It looks the same.

That night I awaken with my eyes burning, my throat raw. The air conditioning unit is inexplicably venting outside air into my room. Even fourteen stories up, my floor is immersed in a constant haze of acrid smoke. Normally, the unit recirculates room air, which is relatively clean.

I fiddle with the thermostat and blower controls, but nothing changes. Finally, I turn it off. It's 85 degrees outside, and the room temperature gradually rises. But it's better to suffer in the heat than to be kept awake by fumes.

I feel as if I'm on the far side of the moon.

Goodbye Bangkok

OF THE TWO SUITS I'VE ORDERED, I ASK THE TAILOR TO SHIP ONE home and bring the other to me at the Tower Inn. Some restaurants and clubs in Europe, particularly France, require formal clothes. I want to be prepared.

I wait into the middle of the afternoon for the suit to arrive, wondering if it will arrive before I have to take the cab to the airport to catch my flight to Paris. Okay, so it's Friday the thirteenth, I realize with a chagrin that feels more like a voodoo spell than a silly superstition. Finally, I call the tailor.

"Had to go to airport today. I send boy up now," she says.

Shortly, the reception desk calls; the suit has arrived.

I put my pack on the back of my chair, my suitcase on my lap, and take a last look around. "Can't say I've had lots of fun," I tell the walls, "but thank you, room, for taking care of me." I roll happily down the long, hot, smoky hallway and take the elevator down.

At the desk, I take the jacket out and try it on. Perfect fit. I put it with the slacks in my backpack.

By now, the guards and porters know me. As I wheelie and bounce down the two steps they laugh with approval, pointing this feat out to each other. One gives me a *thumbs-up*. In an environment unfriendly to wheelchairs, I've proven myself. Their smiles mean everything, and make all of Bangkok's rough edges seem acceptable.

The hotel's specially arranged cab costs only 400 baht. It's an independent, and the car is unmarked. I decide that's okay. I've come to trust the hotel staff. Anyone who would take the hinges off a door for you in the wee hours of the morning is likely to call a reliable cab.

For fifteen minutes we fight congested downtown traffic, then suddenly ramp onto a freeway and speed away.

After we're free of the city's core and the middle-aged driver doesn't have to concentrate so intently upon missing crazy drivers, he chatters almost continuously in brutally inflected pidgin English, pointing out landmarks with one hand while the other hand jerks the wheel back and forth. I catch the word *road* as he points at a freeway under construction, and there is something about water and a big building, but the rest is lost. One thing is clear: he loves his city. Occasionally, I throw in a "Yes!" or a "Really?" and we get along like best friends.

When I begin to see jets taking off and landing in the distance I decide I will survive yet another wild cab ride. He pulls into the terminal and makes sure I'm inside and okay before he screeches off.

I wander around. It's 6 PM, and my flight doesn't leave till 11. There isn't much to do. The shops sell tourist junk: canned and dried Thai food, silk scarves, gems, perfume, wood carvings—most of it hideously overpriced. The liquor is expensive. Even if it were cheap, I'd pass. Both times I've purchased liquor—the Southern Comfort which broke in my bag, and the Port which disappeared with my camera and backpack—disaster has struck.

I discover a KFC. This American food chain seems to have thrived in this part of the world. I nibble at three pieces of greasy chicken, but pass on the greasy fries. It doesn't taste quite right.

At a sundries shop, I buy a sixteen-pack of nappies (their name for disposable diapers.) My bladder is trained (part of hospital rehab) to void when full. I use disposable diapers at night. It's just one of life's little accommodations for someone with paralysis. It works quite well and allows me to do without a more complicated and potentially health-threatening catheter. I'd almost run out, and had no idea how to find a store in downtown Bangkok where I could buy more. Finding them is a great relief.

I think few people understand what people with my kind of paralysis have to do in order to deal with urination. Maybe this is a good time to explain. During the daytime, I have a urinary leg bag attached to a rubber tube. A condom is perforated and attached with a plug, then glued to you-know-what with latex cement. This allows me to engage in normal activities throughout the day. In twenty-five years, I've had relatively few problems with this set-up.

When I was in the hospital, the doctors told me this was the arrangement that spy plane pilots use on long missions. Okay, I was seventeen, and devastated by my spinal-cord injury. But it could be true. Couldn't it? When you wear a pressure suit and are stuck in a cockpit for fifteen hours, taking a whiz must be a challenge. This would solve the problem, at least technically. Whether someone with feeling would be comfortable, I don't know. Thinking that jet jocks use the method made me feel a lot better when I was a kid. Come to think of it, it still does!

Half an hour before the flight, they board me on the 747-400. It's Air France, and is filled with mostly French tourists. As soon as the seat belt light goes out, half the passengers stand to visit other half. Occasionally, someone shouts across the cabin to get a friend's attention. It's nice. It breaks up twelve hours of tedium. Of course, I understand none of it.

After a meal and a movie, the cabin lights dim. People don sleeping masks, insert earplugs, and snuggle beneath thin airline blankets. I luxuriate in the clean dry cabin air and manage to doze in one-hour shifts. In the middle of the night, I ask to be taken by the narrow aisle-chair to the bathroom. I empty my legbag and return to my seat.

MARCH 14

Paris to Rome

PARIS HAS PEA SOUP WEATHER. I'M THE LAST PASSENGER OFF THE
plane, and expect to see my black wheelchair waiting for me at the top of
the ramp. Instead, a rickety chrome chair and a young man in a sharp-
looking suit await.

"Where's my chair?"

"It is being transferred to your connecting flight to Rome, Mr.
Morse."

This is unacceptable. It's an hour until my Rome flight. I could survive, uncomfortably, in this primitive chair. But my concern is the baggage handling system. Too much disappears forever in the roller-ramp
bowels of airports. I'm not going to trust that my wheelchair will get into
the same plane I am taking to Rome. I begin my protest with the *personal
comfort* approach.

"It is like your shoes," I say bluntly. "How would you feel if they
asked you to use the airport's shoes during plane transfers?"

"It is just a short wait; we can take you in this chair directly to your
plane," he replies, polite but insistent. At least his English is good. I count
my blessings.

Still, he's resolute. My personal comfort won't sway him. I switch
tactics. "I need my chair," I say flatly. "An airline once lost my chair. I
can't afford to lose my chair now." I tell him the story of how my chair

once vanished into baggage limbo.

I was attending law school in Illinois during the late seventies. Back then, airlines didn't get too many wheelchair passengers, and there seemed to be no clear protocol. I boarded a flight in Seattle which stopped in Portland and went on to St. Louis. It was January. The mid-west was buried under heavy snow. All I wanted was to get safely back to the dorm at Southern Illinois University. But when I was brought by aisle chair to the aircraft door, instead of my own chair, there was another.

"That's not mine."

"Oh." There was an uncertain pause as the young agent considered his response. "Well, I'm sure yours is down in the hold."

A baggage handler was sent to search. He came back with another chair, not mine either.

"Nope." I said. "Where's my wheelchair?"

The third chair they brought was undoubtedly scrounged from the terminal; jets simply don't carry a compliment of extra wheelchairs. By now, we had a platoon of frantic agents, flight attendants and baggage people, all making calls and assuring me everything would be okay. But they still couldn't find it.

Finally, the harried manager came out from wherever head honchos hide. I'm certain he visualized the headline: *AIRLINE LOSES PASSENGER'S WHEELCHAIR!*

"We will put you up at the airline's expense in the hotel where the crews stay. We will buy your meals. And we *will* find your chair."

Had I been more savvy, I would have asked for a free round-trip ticket. But I just wanted my wheelchair.

They called me an hour later, at the hotel. The chair had been unloaded in Portland and had ended up in the *Lost Baggage* department. It would come on tomorrow's first morning flight.

I was uncomfortable. I had been given a hemiplegic's wheelchair, geared to move by pushing only one rim. It was as disabling for me as it would be to require a backpacker to wear high heels. Out of that experience I resolved to take responsibility for making certain my chair got on and off planes when I did.

He listens patiently, then says: "I will have someone get it for you." He punches out a number on his mobile phone, has a brief conversation in French.

Shortly, my wheelchair appears, and my brief stay at the airport becomes nearly pleasurable.

HALFWAY INTO THE FLIGHT SOUTH TO ROME, THE CLOUDS BREAK. The Italian Alps gleam below like a sea of white-capped waves. They remind me of the Cascade Mountains back home. But Julius Caesar marched his legions across these. Hannibal brought his elephants into their icy majesty. I'm entranced. I stare down until the bright peaks slip over the horizon.

On the ground, a hydraulic lift lowers me from the aft hatch. Two uniformed escorts wait for security to call and okay my transfer. We sit on the tarmac, next to the jet. I'm wearing a long-sleeved shirt, but still feel chilled. I've been in one long summer since May. Fortunately, the sun's out. And after the stifling heat of Bangkok and Singapore, this crisp spring air is refreshing.

The cell phone call comes. I'm loaded into a special wheelchair van. At the terminal, two guards with shoulder-slung machine guns briefly look me over, then move on.

Duncan, a friend I haven't seen since high school, is waiting. He works in Rome, and mutual friends put us back in contact after twenty-five years. It's nice to see a familiar face.

"We'll take the scenic route," he says with a smile as I take my chair apart for the cabby. Duncan gives directions in Italian to the driver, who smiles. "Si Signore!" And we're off, the cabby talking over his shoulder, Duncan translating.

"There's the Forum." "That's the Colosseum." "That spire is St. Peter's." "Here's the Via Veneto." "Over that hill is the Circus Maximus and the palace of the Caesars." "Here's our Embassy." "This park surrounds the Villa Borghesi."

I had no idea how much of an impact Rome would have on me. For every movie, every book, every photograph I've ever seen, there is a *real* place in Rome where it actually happened. I quickly lose track, but it's all still wonderful.

Duncan has booked me into the Jolly Hotel. I'd be welcome at his apartment, but he lives several stories up, and the elevator is too small for my wheelchair. *It's a city full of cracker box elevators*, he emailed me when I was in Melbourne. So we agreed upon a hotel as the best option.

The Jolly's accessibility has remained a question mark until now. But after discovering that my room has a wide bathroom door, and that the marbled bathroom is filled with completely accessible fixtures and a tub in which I can easily shower, I immediately confirm my reservation for the balance of my time in Rome.

As I unpack, Duncan asks, "Have you got enough energy for a walk around the old city this afternoon? And there's a party tonight at the Canadian Embassy, if you want to go." It's 11 AM. I'm completely jazzed. I have no signs of jet-lag. A walk through ancient Rome? An embassy party? They're impossible to resist.

"Sure, but I need to get my feet up for a while." I may not feel jet-lagged, but my feet have swollen during the flights of the past sixteen hours. It's not uncommon, and I've learned to schedule some time to elevate them so the edema can dissipate.

"How's two o'clock sound?"

"Okay."

Duncan leaves. I take a deep breath, congratulate myself on getting this far, then pull two pillows from the queen bed, lay them end-to-end on the floor, and get down and put my feet up on the bed.

I try to doze, but my body refuses to be tired. After an hour of lying on the floor, feeling ridiculous, I get up, shower, dress, and wait for Duncan.

We catch a cab down the Via Veneto, past the American Embassy, and into the old section. Friends warned me about Rome's curbs and cobbles, but I find the city easy to negotiate. The curbs are just inches high; the cobbles have been worn smooth by the shoes of millions of tourists.

Eventually, we end up at the Pantheon. Duncan asked what I *had* to see in Rome. This is it. For me, the Pantheon is the living incarnation of ancient Rome. Built in the second century as a temple housing Rome's gods, and later converted by Christians into a church, it is Rome's oldest functional large structure. For eighteen centuries, the massive dome has survived invasion, earthquake, fire and neglect. You could sleep a thousand on its floor. Oddly, it's roughly the same shape as a nuclear containment dome.

We enter through bronze doors that would easily admit a double-decker bus. "Original, as far as I can tell," Duncan says of these gargantuan gates. The pins holding the doorframe have abraded the stone, and the frame has shifted several inches. But the doors still swing shut every night.

We cross the mosaic floor and stare up at the circle of empty niches where statutes of gods and goddesses once were lodged. I get a chill:

Roman emperors, senators, soldiers and citizens have stood where I now am.

Later, Duncan and I sit at an outdoor cafe, sipping lattes, luxuriating in the afternoon sun. "We're just starting to get nice weather," Duncan says. "Last week, it almost snowed."

We catch a cab back to the Jolly, and I'm finally able to sleep. In two hours, Duncan returns to take me to the party.

I've met some fun-loving people in my time, but the Hash House Harriers take the prize. The Hash is a worldwide social group of people living outside their own countries. It originated when a few out-of-shape embassy employees organized a race to get some exercise. The *Hash House* was where that first group ate; *Harrier*, is for the running. There are now hundreds of chapters. The Hashers have come to Rome to whoop it up tonight and run tomorrow. American, English, Irish, Canadian, Italian, and more, they dance into the night.

It's a toga party. The *raison 'd etre* for this weekend's gathering is a run from the Circus Maximus to the Forum, where CNN will cover the group's re-enactment of the slaying of Julius Caesar. Tomorrow is March 15, also known in the ancient Roman world as the *Ides of March*. Thus, the Roman-style togas.

At 1 AM Duncan comes over. "Maybe you should get some sleep," he says. I can't believe it when he tells me the time. I've been on the go almost forty hours. Duncan's right. If I want to avoid a serious crash, I'd better call it an evening, even though I'm having a blast.

When I reach my room, I take a wonderfully long, hot shower; two days of travel have finally done me in. I eat the chocolate laid on the pillow case and slide between the crisp sheets. I sleep like a rock.

MARCH 15

The Ides of March

THE HASHERS START THEIR MEMORIAL RUN AT NOON. Thirty-five runners in flowing white sheets jog across the Circus Maximus depression and disappear in the direction of the Palatine. It was a little over two thousand years ago that Caesar uttered his famous line, *"Et tu, Brute?"* to Brutus, the spurned suitor of his daughter, Julia, who had instead chosen Pompey the Great. Partly in revenge for not choosing him as a son-in-law, Brutus helped other senators stab Caesar to death. Sure, I've seen the movie and read books about what is arguably the world's most famous assassination. But it sends an entirely different kind of chill up your spine when you are *there where it actually happened.*

I can't run with the group so when they are finally all out of sight I wander up a narrow cobbled street and find a quiet hilltop park in a neighborhood of centuries-old homes. Surrounded by the famous Roman pines, I sit in a small pool of sun. Did Cicero walk here? Claudius? Marcus Antonius?

Sun dappled shadows cast by the tall pines fall across the grass at my feet. Tiny white daisies have sprung up everywhere in the spring-green turf. A wrinkled *nonna* in a black shawl walks slowly past, lost in thought. A young couple, holding hands as they walk slowly across the other side of the park, is engrossed in conversation. A few pottery fragments litter a mound of fresh earth recently tilled for some as-of-yet undecipherable construction project. I pick up one small shard, examine the clear-glazed terra cotta, then reverently put it back down, wondering, *How old?*

Eventually, I roll the few blocks back down to the graveled lot on the edge of the Circus Maximus. The Hashers straggle in by one's and two's.

When everyone has returned a circle is formed. Two members have now attended their first five gatherings and are entitled to receive nicknames under the Hasher's loose set of rules. I watch as they kneel and flour is sprinkled on their heads, then beer is poured on the flour to form a gooey mass. The nickname is an honor that is chosen by some process that I am not privy to. Whoever makes the choices must know something about the person being named because the names can be quite revealing and personal. I am sitting in the circle between two long-time Hashers whose nicknames are *Poison* and *Foreplay*. I watch beer and flour drip down the initiates' heads and necks and onto their shoulders and I'm glad not to be up for initiation on this fine Roman spring day.

Diana, who teaches in Sicily, comes over. We visited at last night's party. "Why don't you come to Sicily?" she asks. "I'm sure we can find a Hasher who'll put you up for a few days. You could visit my school and talk to the kids. They would love it."

I was cautioned about Sicilian crime, particularly theft, but Diana's been there two years and assures me I'll be safe. She also says the weather should be warmer than in the north.

"Send me an email," she says. "Let me know when you're coming. We'll plan from there." That quickly, my travel focus shifts.

MARCH 18

Vatican City

ROMAN DRIVERS ARE CRAZY, ESPECIALLY THE MOPEDS WHICH
weave through traffic at breakneck speed as if there were no tomorrow.
On a trip to Vatican City, I'm starting to cross the street when a motor
scooter (Duncan calls them *motorinis*) comes screaming around a blind
corner, narrowly missing me and several other pedestrians. Five hooded
nuns and I dash across to the safety of the square where the Pope gives
his weekly sermon.

As I approach St. Peters I see no wheelchair ramp, just broad steps.
I sit for a minute, trying to figure out where the disabled entrance is. A
young couple walks up.

"May we help?" he says in a heavy French accent.

"Well ... would you mind carrying me up the steps?"

"How do we do it?"

I show him where to grab the bar in back; his girlfriend grabs the
foot rail. Two other tourists quickly come to assist and I find myself being
carried inside as delicately as if I were a crate of Tiffany glass. They set me
down at the top.

"You are American?" He asks.

"Yes."

"You travel with someone?" Everyone seems to assume this.

"No." I explain my solo trip.

"Call me when you get to Paris," he says enthusiastically. He scribbles a name and a phone number on a slip of paper. I give him the *Wenatchee World's* Internet address so they can read my articles.

St. Peter's makes the Pantheon seem like a Quonset hut. It's alcoves, dedicated to saints and popes and always with huge, ornate statuary, are as large as some churches back home. Even small details can be humbling, like the three ornately carved wooden confessionals along one wall which look ancient enough to have serviced Napoleon's confession. For all I know they might have been around when Joan of Arc was doing her thing.

Until now, I've seen no other wheelchairs in Rome. I've heard that paralyzed people simply stay home. Now I spot several wheelchair-bound individuals, most with MS- and CP-type illnesses. All have escorts; all are praying. Several appear capable of some degree of independence but all are being pushed and coddled. It makes me sad, angry and defensive. I think of Christopher Reeve, who has difficulty breathing, yet continues to direct and act. And the great physicist, Stephen Hawking, unable to communicate with anyone not specially trained to understand his difficult speech, yet still a productive thinker. So much of disability is about the expectations of those around you. It's so hard to be courageous and adventurous when everyone tells you not to be.

I leave St. Peters and head for the Vatican Museum. On the way there I spot a hole-in-the-wall restaurant and stop for lunch. I sit across from a priest in a simple white cassock and order pasta, bread and a small carafe of red wine. As I speak to the waiter the priest glances over, then back to his food. When the waiter is gone he asks politely, "Are you an American?" His English is excellent, almost without accent.

"Yes. And you?"

"Dutch. But I taught psychology at Columbia for several years."

We talk about my project, about Columbia University, about his love for America. We discover a mutual interest in the late Supreme Court Justice William O. Douglas, who attended Columbia Law School, and whose books I collect.

"Good luck with your trip," he says when I leave.

"And you with yours."

What to say about the Vatican Museum? I spend two entirely inadequate hours being overwhelmed by hundreds, no *thousands,* of objects dating back as far as ancient Rome. Gifts from emperors and kings, booty from the Crusades, holy icons. And finally, the Sistine Chapel, filled with gawking tourists surreptitiously taking photographs. I respect the sign and keep my camera in its bag.

There was a recent controversy about whether or not to clean centuries of dirt and soot from Michelangelo's frescos. Now, the cleansing is almost complete. The images are bright, the interplay of colors is sensuous. The fresh-scrubbed cherubs, angels, saints, and the stark countenance of God reaching his finger to spark life into man, assure me that Michelangelo felt joy in his heart as he painted.

MARCH 20

Train to Sicily

FOR THE FIRST TIME, I'LL TRAVEL BY TRAIN IN EUROPE. I ARRIVE forty-five minutes early, just to make certain I have enough time to sort out the details with someone who might not speak English. Inside the huge Roma Termini, I'm directed to a window at the far end. After the agent enters the travel date on my Europass she sends me to platform twelve. I remember Charlie's warning about being gassed on Italian trains; it seems like forever since I sat, sampling glasses of wine with him, in Australia's Hunter Valley.

I pull the black collar of my new denim jacket (purchased in Rome) against the morning cold and read the names stenciled in white block letters on the cars: Messina, Palermo, Syracuse. From the reader board inside the station I know the Syracuse cars will pass through Catania which is where I'm headed.

The platform clock reads 7:45; I've plenty of time before the 8:15 scheduled departure. I would board immediately, but there are three steps and no one to lift me up. A porter, brakeman or engineer will certainly come along. I find a spot where the sun pools on the black asphalt, set my backpack and suitcase down, and wait.

Ten minutes later, I'm becoming concerned. Most of the passengers have boarded. I pick up my luggage and start rolling up toward the engine, hoping to find someone who can help me up.

It's not until I reach the front of the train, 200 yards away, that I find three conductors, smoking and chatting amiably in Italian. *"Scuzi, signores,* does anyone speak English?"

"A little," one says. "What you need?"

"I'm going to Catania. I need help getting on the car."

They have a brief discussion before they pitch their cigarettes. Two of the men escort me back down the length of the train, one talking on his mobile phone as we go. He says someone will meet us with a wheelchair lift.

We walk by a pretty Japanese girl who asks for help in what sounds like very adequate Italian. It makes me feel ignorant. One of the men stays with her.

When we reach the Syracuse car, we wait. I'm assured that a lift is coming. The other conductor rejoins us. We wait. Nothing remotely like a lift is coming from either direction.

My confidence fades. I look up at the clock and realize the train leaves in five minutes. We are now the *only* people still on the platform. The conductors are nervously consulting their wristwatches, looking disgusted, and mumbling what must be expletives.

Finally, they confer, overtones of frustration transcending our language barrier. "We lift you on," the English-speaking conductor says. They way-lay a baggage handler as he walks by and he is quickly assigned to lift the heavy end. Within seconds, I'm inside.

Unfortunately, there is a stencil of a smoking cigarette on the glass door; it's a smoking car. But I'm far too late to protest. A middle-aged priest and an elderly nun are already in the six-seat compartment, but neither has lit up. Maybe I'll get lucky. I smile at them, he says something in Italian, I say, "I'm American. I don't speak Italian. Do you speak English?" He smiles, "No, signore."

Within two minutes the train is moving. There is none of the herky-jerky I've come to expect from older trains; the tracks are obviously well laid and maintained, the engineer highly skilled. Our progress through the rail yard, through the suburbs and out into the countryside is smooth and quick.

A conductor comes for tickets. He studies the priest's and I catch the meaning of only one of his words. "*Due*," he says repeatedly, which means *two* in Italian. The priest has a ticket for second class; this is first class. They politely argue, but the conductor is unrelenting. The priest finally stands; the conductor smiles apologetically. The nun leaves with the priest.

The conductor pulls a role of blue tape from his pocket. I've already taken the wheels off my wheelchair and stowed them under my seat. The frame, which compacts relatively small and is in no one's way since there is no one else in the cabin, is in the seat opposite. But he motions that he has to put it on the overhead rack. He lifts it up and proceeds to tape it to the rack in four places.

I keep trying to get him to understand that I'll eventually have to use the bathroom; it's just down the hall and accessible to me if I can use my chair. He seems to understand and I believe I've gotten my point across. At least he smiles a lot, and nods affirmatively as I talk.

He finishes taping and leaves. I never see him again.

In the countryside beyond Rome, the small orchards of peach, pear and apple trees are covered with pink and lavender blossoms. New shoots of broccoli and cauliflower nudge aside freshly plowed soil. Yellow and white wild flowers brighten ditches. Trees near the many small farmhouses are already hung with ripe oranges. Fields ripple with new grain and alfalfa. And everywhere are grape vines and olive trees.

I imagine the time of Julius Caesar. Little would have changed, except the roads would be stone instead of asphalt, and no power or phone lines would be strung along the roads. The ancient stone aqueduct we now parallel would be well maintained instead of two-thirds fallen down. Mule carts, rather than trucks, would be carrying goods and produce into the city.

We pass through Naples and Salerno and climb into a range of rocky hills more suited to goats and sheep than to farming. The train passes through dozens of short tunnels. The tracks curve and twist and climb and fall and our speed drops by half, to around thirty-five mph.

After several narrow valleys, the track resumes a course along the coastline. Occasionally we pass a seaside cove filled with red-tile-roofed bungalows fronting empty beaches. The Mediterranean stretches clear and blue to the horizon and serene little waves wash up against the golden sand. One or two colorful rowboats ride out in the bay carrying solitary fishermen who hold their poles waiting for the next fish. And suddenly there is darkness as the train penetrates the next tunnel.

In the four hours since Rome, no one has come to check on me. I'm disgusted with the blue tape that binds my wheelchair out of reach and reinforces my isolation. I've fortunately brought an empty plastic drink bottle in my suitcase and have twice drained my leg bag into it. It's now full. I need to get to the bathroom.

Two police officers come down the hall and glance in the window to my compartment. I waive at the woman but she ignores me and they walk on.

Ten minutes later a man in a porter's uniform strolls by. I waive furiously and he pokes his head in. For two minutes I try to convey that I need the wheelchair down from the rack. Finally, he says "*Momento*," and leaves. He doesn't return.

Two more conductors come down the hallway and I motion them

into my cabin. We have trouble communicating. They leave. My leg bag situation is now desperate; if I pee again, I'll have to let some of it out on the carpet.

A few minutes later a conductor who speaks a tiny bit of English arrives. After five minutes of my pleading, almost to the point of tears, he rips the four strands of blue tape and lifts my frame down. But he still doesn't seem to understand *why* I need it.

"I have to use the rest room," I say. He spreads his hands and shakes his head. "Bathroom," I say. He shakes his head. "Lavatorio?" He shakes his head again. There comes a time when you have to yield your dignity in order to get something done. I reach down and point to the now-full drink bottle on the floor, then pull up my pant leg and show him my full leg bag.

"Ah!" he says, smiling. He reaches for the bottle, then takes it out into the hall. I hear first flushing, then water in a sink. He brings it back clean.

When he's gone, I empty my leg bag into the bottle.

I can now lie down and catch a bit of rest. I lift the armrests and stretch out. Three seats together are just enough; my soles touch the far side, the tip of my head the near. I drift off for an hour in the pleasantly warm, gently swaying car.

We reach the ferry dock at 4 PM. Messina is just visible across the choppy strait. I'd like to get off the train and take a look around but without an interpreter to find out when the train goes onto the ferry, plus someone reliable to lift me back into my car, it's impossible.

After an hour's wait the train trundles forward, then backs down a spur that extends onto the dock. The last four cars inch inside the huge ferry; the train lurches as they uncouple; we retreat twenty yards. The process repeats. I'm in the third segment to go inside.

In the immense steel cavern of the ferry's interior there are no windows or openings. The power in my car goes off and I'm left in shadowy darkness. I lie down during the half-hour crossing, soothed by the powerful throb of the engines, wondering what it looks like from the deck.

Things move fast in Messina. The train is split in two. Our Syracuse section ambles down the eastern coast, skirting the flanks of Mt. Etna. Above ancient ruins and wild grapes on the slopes to our right I can see that fresh ash limes the conical peak. Wisps of venting gas are visible near the summit, leaving no doubt that this is a very active volcano.

The tracks hold to the coast and I can see fishermen in small boats pulling in their nets a few hundred yards off the gravel beaches, carefully picking fish out as the nets come over the gunnels. In the tiny Sicilian villages that front the shore the paint on houses is peeling and the roofs have many broken tiles. In the worst cases the walls are crumbling at the corners. Times are tougher here than on the mainland.

Announcements on the train's loudspeaker system are quite naturally in Italian. Each time the scratchy voice rattles off the next stop I listen for *Catania.* We are in and out of these little train stations almost without coming to a full stop. We never seem to pause long enough for me to negotiate the hallway and make it to the door with my luggage, much less attract someone's attention for assistance. I'm getting nervous about being stuck on the train and winding up in way southern Sicily.

Finally, three uniformed men come to my car. One speaks English.

"Are you for Catania?"

"Yes."

"We will help you."

"How long will it be before we get there?"

"It is soon." They leave.

Two stops later I hear *Catania* over the speaker. My escort appears and one picks up my bags and to my surprise a special wheelchair lift is waiting on the platform. For once they seem to be well organized.

The lift jostles its rubber bumpers against the train doorway and I edge out onto the narrow tracks and a young agent grips the chair frame until we are safely onto the platform.

Two uniformed station men take over. The younger one picks up my luggage; the middle-aged fellow begins to push me.

"I can push," I say, putting my hands on the rims. But he either doesn't understand or doesn't believe that I actually want to push myself. He keeps shoving. I remember that people in wheelchairs here are considered invalids. I yield.

The track crossing for luggage carts is at the far end of this platform which is the second platform out from the main station. We set out for it but when we arrive we stop and the men get into a lively discussion which is apparently about how best to push me down and across the rails. They must be debating whether to carry the chair, or risk pushing me from behind. I see my chance and quickly flip into a wheelie and zoom over the rails and up the ramp on the other side before either can react.

I spin around and give them a cheesy grin. Both men stand frozen, stunned. Slowly, they take deep breaths, look at each other, and laugh. The older one now chastises his junior in an amused tone. They shake their heads, come over to my side of the tracks, and the old guy says something to me and then pats me on the shoulder. Neither man attempts to push me as we move toward the station house. I cherish the victory. Who knows? It may make them think differently about someone they know who is in a wheelchair.

It's 7 PM. My train has arrived an hour early. Someone named Rex is supposed to meet me, but no one approaches as I look around expectantly. Having no idea what Rex looks like, I find a cement column in the waiting area, back up to it, and put a bag on either side of my chair. My denim jacket with its nylon liner barely keeps me comfortable as cold air wafts through the building.

The terminal is busy. The mechanical reader board shows trains arriving from Rome, Palermo, Messina, Salerno. Darkly complected Sicilians, dressed in black and gray coats and scarves and hats and gloves, are streaming through the station. I feel their eyes upon me. I'm clearly not Sicilian with my medium brown hair and light skin. To say nothing of the wheelchair which is even more of an anomaly here than it was in Rome.

Shortly before 7:30 a man walks up. He is short, stout, middle-aged, with graying hair and a light complexion.

"Are you Rex?" I ask.

"No, I'm Bob," he says with a Texan accent.

"Oh."

"Diane couldn't contact Rex. So you're going to stay at our house. Can you ride a Harley?"

"A what?"

"A Harley."

"You mean a motorcycle?"

"Yes."

"No."

"You sure?"

I can't tell if he's joking or serious. He sure looks serious. Even if I could get on a motorcycle, where would my chair and bags go?

"Positive," I reply.

"Oh! Well, my wife will be here in a few minutes." He smiles and his amused look confirms he was pulling my leg. "You can go in her car," Bob says. It turns out that Bob is the grand mahout of the local Hash chapter. If I were the one to assign him a nickname it would most certainly be … *Joker.*

MARCH 21

Soldiers' Kids

BOB AND ANITA WERE BURGLED LAST MONTH. IT'S HARD TO believe. They live in a house built of foot-thick brick and surrounded by a ten-foot-high cement wall with glass shards imbedded on top. Their windows have thick iron bars and steel shutters and during the daytime the landlord patrols the neighborhood. American jails are hardly more secure. Yet thieves flattened the glass atop the wall, climbed over, and used a log to pound a hole into the house. They took a stereo, a television and some of Anita's jewelry.

It's depressing to have to lock up at night.

Driving on Sicilian roads is yet another frightening reality. Cars routinely cross the centerline to pass on rural roads and it doesn't seem to matter if there is oncoming traffic. I have white knuckles and sweaty palms as I sit beside Anita, driving toward the villaggio, a small seaside village, where she and Bob live. In the space of ten miles we are repeatedly forced onto the shoulder. There is even a full-sized bus that passes us from behind and continues to pass cars ahead, nearly forcing every other vehicle into the ditch. We are doing seventy-five.

"This is the fourth-most-deadly stretch of road in the world," Anita says calmly, as though it's a bonus just to survive.

The next morning I go to the school on the military base. The kids are enthusiastic, if for no other reason than it breaks up the monotony of their routine. I meet with three groups, two in the morning, one in the afternoon. By the end of my day I have a new appreciation for a teacher's workday. It's been non-stop question and answer. But I also feel regenerated. I've gotten to talk not just about my travel, but also about wheelchair life in general. I'm getting my story across to young, impressionable minds, and most of these kids have had no direct experience with someone in a chair.

Several of the kids come up to me after each session and shake my hand, telling me they'll buy my book. And that feels good. If you can interest a child, you know you've gotten through. If I do nothing else in Sicily, these sessions will make the trip here worthwhile.

March 21

A Picnic

On Saturday, Anita takes me to the outdoor market in Paterno, a thirty-minute drive from the house. Along the street and in the square the day stalls sell everything from bolts of cloth to shoes to fish and olives. I see no other obvious tourists. It is still spring and only the locals are out. My wheelchair makes me stand out but only the small children stare.

We walk the length of the street, looking for a particular vendor, but Anita can't find him. Giving up, she leads me to where chickens are spitted and roasting on a charcoal rotisserie. We buy two birds and then fill out the impromptu smorgasbord with a pound of spicy green and black olives, orange soda, and a flat loaf of olive bread.

Back in the car we battle through the narrow streets, fending off drivers with blaring horns who must be chronically hurried or eternally peeved. On the hill at the center of town, beside the crumbling walls of a twelfth-century Norman castle, with a view of Mt. Etna haloed by cloud and the red tile roofs of the city below, we spread a picnic.

MARCH 23

Sick Again

I ATTEND SCHOOL ON MONDAY, BUT I'VE CAUGHT WHAT THE locals are calling the *Catania Crud*. A hacking cough cuts my energy and my voice becomes rougher throughout the day. By the time Anita takes me home when the school lets out I have a mild case of laryngitis and my phlegm is brown.

As if to pile insult upon injury, Tuesday brings a heavy rain and biting cold. I'm forced by my illness to remain at home. The house has no central heat. It's built for summer. Heat comes only from a fireplace and portable kerosene heaters. The fumes from these heaters only aggravate my throat and sinuses. I barely sleep at night, further sapping my energy.

After everyone has left for the workday I struggle up and take a long hot shower that helps ease my aches. I then turn off the kerosene heaters and let the morning fire burn out. My lungs are finally fume-free.

I type at my computer, bundled in a long-sleeved cotton pullover and coat, sipping microwave coffee. I fantasize about Hemingway in Paris while he wrote *A Moveable Feast*. Fuel was expensive and money scarce so Hemingway hung out in cafes where fires were kept burning. I now wish I had a cozy cafe in which to sip wine and write.

I have decided to leave Sicily. I'll take tomorrow's 2 PM train from Catania to Palermo, arriving at 6 PM, then catch the 10 PM overnight ferry from Palermo to Genoa.

THE KIDS AREN'T MY SOLE REWARD IN SICILY. I ALSO GAIN SOME insight on what it's like to be stationed in a foreign country. I learn how precious the military base is for our service men and women. The base offers American-style stores, a bowling alley, a theater, and people who share your cultural values and speak your language.

I see pride in the soldiers' faces and I realize how significant their sacrifices are. They undergo scrutiny by foreigners, fear of terrorism, and a loss of much of their privacy. Nothing can be taken for granted. The Navy guards at the base gate are deadly serious and their Italian counterparts, carrying sub-machine guns, are even more so. Even my wheelchair, which is normally a ticket through security with little hassle, makes no difference. Each day I have to be personally sponsored onto the base by either Bob or Anita, and the guards make me start my laptop computer each time I come and they hold onto my passport until I leave.

I won't soon forget this insider's view.

MARCH 25

A Ship to Genoa

ON WEDNESDAY A COLD RAIN LASHES ACROSS THE PLATFORM AND a gusting wind penetrates my cuffs and collar as I leave the railway station house to cross the tracks so I can board the train to Palermo. The agent assigned to help me reaches out to push, but if I let him take charge it will turn into a slow process and we'll both get soaked. So I race off before he can grab ahold of my chair, rain plastering my face, with him chugging along behind and probably quite perplexed about what to do. My reward is that I'm not completely drenched when I finally reach the shelter of the far platform.

When he catches up to me he's out of breath. He lights up a cigarette and takes several deep drags. No doubt they'll talk about the *speedy American* for a long time to come.

It's a small train, much like the Geyserland Express, except not so stylish. They lift me on quickly. This time my chair remains assembled and sits across the aisle within easy reach. I pull off the wet denim jacket and drape it over the wheelchair. The inner nylon shell has remained dry and warm. I reach to feel my legs under my damp cotton pants; they're chilled. I remove my shoes and roll up my pants, massaging warmth back into each leg.

As we pull out, rain pounds against the windows. All along the harbor waves hammer against the seawall and spew white foam high into the

231

air. It feels like January.

We leave the Bay of Catania and climb into the hills towards the spine of the island. The wind and rain taper off as we move into the rounded mountains. Orange groves ripe with fruit and olive trees and vineyards appear. The shells of ancient stone houses often lie like shadows nearby newer homes that have been built to replace them. There is no sign of industry or mining. It's easy to imagine that farming has gone on here for thousands of years.

As we approach the center of the island a thin blue band edges the horizon. Apple and pear trees bloom pink and white and fields are filled with the knee-high greens of grain and alfalfa. Clusters of tiny yellow daisies are everywhere. Prickly pear cactus tangles up in great masses that spread out beside the tracks. Cows and sheep graze the rolling grasslands and are often herded by a man with a staff and a dog or two.

Our four cars and engine pause at every town to exchange a few passengers. Everyone has the same brown-black hair and dark complexions. Most smoke. They seem to speak as much with their hands as with their mouths.

No one approaches me. This isn't a tourist route and it's not the season when the more adventurous tourists would choose to take the train. Add the wheelchair to the picture and I'm clearly an alien.

I'm tired, but not exhausted. I've got a drippy nose and a loose cough. At least the phlegm is coming up freely, and the fever and the creepy feeling deep in my lungs are both gone. If I can get a good night's sleep on the ferry I think I'll be fully on the mend.

After we crest the spine of the island and start down toward the ocean the clouds descend, the rain thickens, and the wind becomes shrill and relentless. By the time we reach the Mediterranean there is nearly a gale blowing in off the water. Heavily dressed tradesmen who now board our train for their commute home have their hands stuffed deep in their pockets and their caps pulled tight over their ears.

Palermo is better equipped to handle wheelchairs than Catania. A lift is waiting for me in a large shed that shelters the train from the weather. I go directly into the large heated station house.

I spot a crowded steam-table cafe at the center of the station and go in and order a bowl of macaroni with a red sauce and what is described to me as *beefa steaka* which turns out to be thick slices off a baron of beef that is heavily seasoned with pepper and rosemary. The hearty food and a glass of red wine are a good tonic for the weather and my cold.

After dinner I venture into the darkness outside the stationhouse and hail a cab. The rain has let up a little but the wind remains strong.

The ferry I'm to take came to my attention when someone overheard my plans and mentioned it. A travel agent on the Base who spoke both English and Italian booked a cabin on the ferry and also booked me into hotel rooms in Genoa and Cannes which are supposedly wheelchair accessible. Since it's still off-season the bookings came easy. But she warned me that during the Easter holiday season which begins in two weeks the rooms and trains will be packed.

Boarding of the *Fantasy* ferry isn't scheduled till 8 PM but when the man running the show on the docks sees my wheelchair he lets me on immediately. While other passengers are forced to wait in cars and cabs, or cringe from the northern wind on the dock, I'm escorted into the warm marbled lobby where I check in with the woman behind the sweeping wood counter. Chalk another mark up for being in a wheelchair.

She calls a crewman who scans my ticket, then grabs my bags. "We'll put you in a good room in the middle of the ship," he says as we walk to the elevator. "It's going to be a rough crossing." I'm not concerned. The ship is huge and as we walk down the hallway it is dead still. Could it be that much worse beyond the breakwater?

The room they put me in is exceptional. The shower has a fold-down seat; the sink's easy to pull up to; there are plenty of grab bars. And I've been upgraded to an outside cabin. I have a window!

I take a hot shower and, before the other passengers begin to board, crawl under the covers.

I later have a dream that things are moving around the cabin. Lamps and suitcases are being tossed about.

I'm suddenly jostled awake and I feel the ship rolling beneath me. I hear a *cha-cha-cha-chunk* and feel the hull crash through the water. To my relief, when I turn on the bedside light, there is just one moving object: a cabinet drawer is banging open and closed. I wedge my chair against it.

For the next half hour I try to decide whether being rocked (I'm lying cross-cabin, with my feet toward the port) is pleasant or aggravating. My stomach votes by remaining calm. From then on I sleep like a log.

Next morning, the elevators have been turned off. I call the desk and am assured that a technician will fix them immediately. A purser knocks shortly, apologizes, and takes me to the breakfast bar. "This man is our guest," he tells the hostess. "Treat him to whatever he wants." After a cappucino and a croissant, I check the elevators. They're working.

Exploring the ship is less exciting than I imagined. The piano bar and the main restaurant are closed. The *Casino* turns out to be a dozen slot machines and a video arcade corner for kids. The TV in the lounge is, naturally, in Italian, and hearing the news in a foreign language is less than entertaining.

The sea is calmer this morning and as the day progresses it becomes almost placid. But the storm from last night has still held us up and we arrive at 8 PM rather than 6 PM.

Genoa is dark and cold. Those of us needing cabs wait to one side as cars and trucks stream down the ferry ramp. Again, the wheelchair prevails, and I'm given the first available cab.

We ascend a series of switchbacks into the city, which is terraced against the steep foothills of the Apennines. Trekking Genoa in a wheelchair would be a chore, particularly since there are no curb cuts. It makes Seattle or San Francisco seem easy by comparison.

The hotel is on an angled corner two miles from the waterfront. A middle-aged desk clerk who speaks English checks me in. We go to the elevator to ride up to the room but it is one of those classic *cracker boxes* like the one in Duncan's apartment building back in Rome. My chair won't fit. I'm too tired to be concerned. I see an immediate solution.

"Have you got an office chair I can ride up on in the elevator?"

The clerk walks back to the registration desk and wheels out an office chair out from behind the counter. "Will this work, Signore?"

"Yes."

"Do you want to go up now?"

I'm hungry and there is no sense in making the elevator ride twice.

"Is there a restaurant nearby?"

"Yes. Do you want to eat now?"

"Yes."

He takes me around the corner to a small bistro, packed with wooden chairs and tables with checkered tablecloths.

I tell the *maître de*, who turns out to be the owner, that I'm short of lira. "American dollar is always good here!" he says enthusiastically. This leads to a story about his youth following WWII when American GI's were kind to his family. Fifty years later he still remembers chocolate bars, Spam and American cigarettes. "Americans! You the best!"

After a bowl of vegetable soup and a leg of roast chicken I return to the hotel, escorted by the cook whom the owner tells, "Make sure he is safe."

The office chair works just fine in the elevator; they bring my wheel-chair up the steps and have it waiting for my transfer.

The room is large and posh but the bathroom door is too narrow. "No problem," I tell the manager. I point to a side chair. "Just put that in the doorway." The legs are metal, and a thick pad covers the seat. I can transfer onto it and scoot around on the bathroom's polished tile.

MARCH 27

Genoa to Cannes

THE NEXT MORNING I'M TOLD THE FRENCH RAIL WORKERS HAVE gone on strike. I can catch a train as far as the last town on the Italian Riviera, Ventimiglia, but from there I'm on my own to figure out how to complete the trip to Cannes.

"Maybe you can take a bus or a cab?" the manager suggests. But I remember last night's short ride cost $10. A forty-mile fare would be a fortune. But the bus sounds workable.

He calls the station, makes arrangements for me to take the train to Ventimiglia, and inquires about the bus. He reports there is a bus covered by my Europass that I can take from Ventimiglia to Cannes.

The station is just a short cab ride away. Unlike Catania there is no convenient baggage cart ramp between the platforms, just steps. Two young men escort me to a freight lift. The rough wooden platform creaks and clunks as we sink down. After a short walk through an arched cement tunnel, we ride another decrepit lift to a second platform, walk to the end, and take another lift down. Another tunnel, another lift, and we finally come up onto the Ventimiglia platform.

The March air is crisp and I couldn't ask for better scenery. The surrounding hills are crowded with ancient villas. On a far hill sits a castle. New green leaves cloak the trees. I pull my black coat close and appreciate the sun on my face.

The train lumbers in and stops with a squeal of steel on steel. My helpers load me on, then with broad smiles refuse the tip I offer. I wish I could understand what they say to each other as they walk down the platform. "Traveling alone in a wheelchair!" is my guess. And it makes me smile, too.

It takes three hours to reach Ventimiglia. It turns out there is no bus to Cannes, but the strike is supposed to end at 5 PM and the regularly scheduled train will depart at 5:24. I have four hours.

From the steps of the station I spot a crowd at the far end of the street. I find someone who speaks English.

"What's that?" I point toward the people milling about.

"The Friday market."

Now that's more like it! I'm close enough to the end of my trip to pick up a little extra something for a souvenir.

At a French sidewalk cafe I lunch on sliced meats, bread, fillet of sole, wine and chocolate-vanilla ice cream. Then I'm off in search of black dress shoes among the hundreds of day stalls. Even the bargains here are expensive compared to Singapore and Bangkok. But I eventually find a pair I like at a reasonable price.

I catch a few people staring at me. Even here, an active person in a wheelchair is an anomaly. I should have a T-shirt printed up: GET USED TO IT!

The train to France leaves on time. The porters stick me in a small cabin with no seats. It's apparently used for luggage. But at Monte Carlo it suddenly fills with young French workers on their way home. Casino employees? Several have bicycles and we all jostle to find enough space. There are eighteen of us in about seventy-five square feet. One asks me a question in French. I shake my head, lamely saying, "No parle Francais." Two women smile politely but no one speaks French to me again and no one volunteers anything in English.

It takes another hour to get to Cannes. By now, only four of us remain. As we near the stop I ask one fellow if he speaks English.

"A little."

"I need help down at Cannes."

"I get off before but I will ask." He walks into the next car, then returns. "Someone will come back."

At Cannes two men appear from the next car to lift me down. It's a good thing, for the train pulls away after only a brief pause, and no one from the Cannes station shows up before it's gone. Had I not asked, I'd now be on my way to Nice.

I sit with my luggage, not sure what to do next. Someone from the station was supposed to come. It's chilly and my head cold seems to be coming back.

After five minutes a train employee walks up and escorts me across the tracks, through the station, and to the cab rank.

The Cristal Hotel was booked by the travel agent. Whereas the Genoa room wasn't disabled-friendly by any stretch of the imagination, the Cristal's room is very accessible. The one exception is that I'll be relegated to showering while sitting in the bathtub. It's okay. I've done that several times. Besides, a long hot bath would be a wonderful way to erase the chill from the station. There is even a small package of mineral salts in the basket on the bathroom counter.

March 29

Cannes

When is it time to go home? It is time to go home when that little voice inside your head tells you your time is up. This is much the same voice that tells you to exercise regularly, eat healthy food, not indulge your vices too often, and to observe all of the other do's and don'ts we often deny until some kind of damage is done.

Still, it's hard to bite the bullet. I had so looked forward to visiting Spain. Yesterday, I anguished over my decision to return to the US, and finally took solace in a gourmet dinner at the hotel restaurant that included a carafe of red wine. This morning I took a walk and went shopping at the Sunday market. I bought a wedge of Brie, an orange and a banana, and had an impromptu brunch near a table where a fishmonger was filleting sole. The French were out in force on Sunday and the women were dressed to kill. I'll not soon forget the old gal dressed in violent shades of green and orange and wearing a black pillbox hat and walking a miniature poodle who peed on everything he could lift a leg at.

This is a lovely sunny morning in the mid-sixties but my mind is preoccupied with whether to leave or not. And then it comes clear. I've accomplished what I set out to do: have a grand adventure traveling solo around the world in my wheelchair. Would it make the trip any more valid if I spent additional time in Europe? No. I'd have more adventures, but the overall project is complete … if I want it to be. And I do.

Sipping a latte at a sidewalk café as noon approaches I think it through again to make sure I haven't missed something. I reach the same conclusion. It is time to go home.

Back at the hotel the receptionist books a seat for me on the *TGV* train to Paris tomorrow afternoon and a room in downtown Paris for one night. Tomorrow, I'll call and see if British Airways can reserve me a seat on a flight to Seattle the following day.

I'm immediately relieved and actually excited about packing my two suitcases tomorrow morning. I can finally dump stuff I've kept *just in case* (like an extra bottle of contact lens solution.) No more bulging bags. I'm about to go streamline.

This experience has become more for me than proving that a disabled person can have a good time circling the earth alone. I've discovered how much people mean to me. I've been forced to relinquish control, to ask for help, and to admit that I'm stubborn and compulsively independent. I thought the change in me would be a toughening. I think, rather, that the experience has softened me up.

MARCH 30

I Sure Wish I Spoke French

I'M LAZY ON MY LAST MORNING IN CANNES. AT THE TOP FLOOR restaurant I have brioche, croissants and coffee, while I enjoy the sunlight streaming in the windows, knowing that for my 1:17 train I need to be there only half an hour early.

My digital camera batteries are low. I want to buy new AA cells so I can take pictures on the train. So when I see the desk clerk it's the first question on my mind.

"Good morning, Messieur," says the beautiful woman at the front desk.

"Bonjour, Mademoiselle. Is there a shop nearby where I can buy batteries for my camera?"

"Oui. There is a shop just around the corner. But when is your train?"

"Not till one-seventeen. I've got over an hour."

"But Messieur. It is already one o'clock!"

I feel instant panic. But I'm certain my clock was set correctly and it read 11:55 when I left my room.

"We changed to daylight savings time last night," she says.

"Oh shit!" I could have chosen better words. "Can you get me a cab right away?" And then I forget propriety and say "Shit!" a couple more times. And then, "I had no idea," but she isn't listening. Bless her she's on the phone.

The taxi arrives in five of the longest minutes of my life. He would make any New York cabby proud: we pull up in front of the station at 1:10. I tip heavily and hurry inside, almost dropping my suitcase with the precious computer inside, all the while cursing quietly. I should have gotten up earlier. I should have checked with the clerk about my departure time. But how was I to know? And if I had listened to local television and heard the announcement to set clocks back for daylight savings time I wouldn't have understood it anyway. I didn't even know they had daylight savings time in France!

There's a long line at the counter. I have four minutes.

I spot two men in uniforms standing near a pile of luggage. They listen to my urgent plea for help in getting on the train, then point toward a small room off the platform.

"Pardon, monsieur," I say to the man inside the room. "No parle Francais. I need to get on the train. I'm late."

The slender man in his forties ignores me.

"Pardon, monsieur!" He looks up with exasperation. Slowly he stands, puts down his cigarette, walks to me.

"I must get on the train to Paris."

"Do you have a ticket?" he asks. I hand him my Europass.

"Not this." He hands it back as if it were a grocery list. "You need a ticket." He points toward the terminal lobby.

"I don't have any other ticket," I reply, my frustration surging up inside.

"You need a ticket," he says firmly. Down the tracks, the sleek nose of the *TGV* is pulling in smoothly alongside the platform.

"I must get on the train!" I feel like crying, begging, anything. He sighs, looks as if he wishes he'd stayed in bed that morning. He certainly knows that if I take the time to go get a ticket the train will leave without me. Passengers are already getting on and off.

"We must talk to the controller. Come with me." He gets on his portable phone and angrily utters a few words of French.

We walk to the front of the train and meet with an older man in a uniform. They have a heated conversation, throwing occasional glances at me. I try to look as pathetic and repentant as I feel. *Dumb American,* I keep thinking. *For God's sake I'm just a Dumb American! And I'm in a wheelchair! And I can't speak French. So please let me on this train.*

Both men finally turn to me.

"Come with me," the controller says briskly. We walk back down the platform to the fourth car; a wheelchair lift is already being backed up to it.

"Thank you," I say. "You are wonderful, Monsieur. You are a wonderful man." He stops looking put out. But he doesn't smile.

I quickly discover that I am in Second Class, even though my Europass is First Class. I don't care. I would settle for the luggage car. I am barely in my seat when the train pulls out of the station.

Second Class is actually better than any economy airline seat I've ever had. And it's perfectly set up for wheelchairs. One of the two seats on my side of the car folds up so my wheelchair can remain beside me. The cushions are deep, the seat broad, and I discover the luxury of an electric recline button. The aisle is wide enough for my chair. At the end of the car there is a handicapped-accessible bathroom. What do they add for First Class? Hot towels and chocolates?

For half an hour we snake along track cut into rock and cliff. A progression of red-roofed mansions ornament the cliffs fronting the Mediterranean.

Then at the city of Nice the tracks turn north. At first there are vineyards, all manicured like prized gardens. Then castles on far-off cliffs and fort-like towns atop rounded hills and skirted by stone walls. The tracks now have few bends and our speed increases.

After two hours the vineyards are replaced by orchards, which eventually give way to fields where white cattle graze. Finally, there are just rolling fields of green grain and occasional villages. We are now doing at least 150 but the cabin is whisper-quiet. Out my window I watch a second set of rails and can't detect even a quiver of deviation they are so well laid. Impressive.

The weather slowly deteriorates as we head north. The Riviera was sunny. But by the middle of France a high, gray overcast prevails. In Paris, rain threatens, and the temperature is in the low fifties.

MARCH 31

Homeward Bound

BY NOW, MY MOMENTUM TOWARD HOME IS HUGE. BUT THERE IS A problem. My ticket on British Airways from Heathrow to Seattle is for May 5. It is only March 31 so I'm more than a month ahead of schedule.

Once in my hotel room I try calling British Airways but they are closed. So I get on the Internet and find a flight with open seats to take me from Paris to London tomorrow morning. I then try to book it but the system won't accept my credit card.

In the morning I reach British Airways and am happy to learn a seat is still available.

At 10:45 my plane leaves Charles deGaul Airport, landing at Heathrow in thirty-five minutes. Now for the real challenge: getting a flight home.

Heathrow is a huge place that goes on forever. But at least everyone speaks English. A pleasant fellow takes me through security and then to the correct terminal and the British Airways desk. They wait-list me on the 1:15 PM flight, but I am told that it's spring break for students and the prospects are dim. "We'll get you on if we can," the woman running the counter assures me. They move me to the front of the list, but it doesn't help; no seats come open.

"Is there a seat open in First Class that I can upgrade to?" I'm hoping they'll just offer it to me. But no such luck.

"Sure," she says.

"How much?"

She gives me an astronomical figure in English pounds. It comes to around $9,000.

"Wow," is the only comment I can make.

"Sorry," she says.

"Look," I offer. "If I can just exchange my ticket for another economy seat I'll take anything to the west coast of North America."

She nods and heads off in search of a flight, then returns shortly.

"Canadian has a flight to Calgary at three-thirty. We can wait-list you if you want."

"I'll take it. What are my chances?"

"A little better. But it's over-booked. It depends upon who shows up."

"Okay. Let's try it."

A seat opens up and they dash me through Customs to the departure gate at the last moment. For the first time in my life I'm the last to board an aircraft.

My seat companion is an Irishman in his seventies. We talk about WWII, his children and grandchildren. Eight hours pass quickly and now I'm in Calgary.

I find the Horizon Air counter. A flight to Seattle with connections to Wenatchee is available ... for $450. Count your blessings, I tell myself. I hand her my Mastercard.

On March 31, five months and a week after I left, my turbo-prop plane touches down at Wenatchee. My neighbors, Chris and Tammy, are waiting in the small terminal. Outside it has cooled into the forties. Stars fill the sky. The Big Dipper and Polaris the North Star are reassuringly familiar.

They have purchased a new butterscotch-colored Volvo since I left nearly half a year ago. Do I like it? Yeah, it's beautiful. But other questions press on my mind. Has anyone I know died? They don't think so. How was the winter? Mild and with not much snow. Is there anything new in our neighborhood? No. The big excitement has been the birth of their first grandson. How was the trip? What did I do? I promise to give them all the particulars after I've settled back into a routine.

In Chelan my house still stands. My car has a thick coat of dust. The heat registers in my bedroom emit a musky smell when I turn them up.

I sort my travel stuff into piles, retrieve the mouse traps (and two desiccated mice), decide the box of unopened mail is too huge to tackle tonight, check to make sure none of my canned fruit has exploded, turn on the faucets until the water stops running brown, and run two loads of laundry.

It's funny being gone for this long. It's like awakening from a coma and discovering that everything has changed just a little.

Near midnight I crawl under the covers. My body clock is messed up. I was in Paris twenty-four hours ago. It feels like morning. Yet, in my own bed, surrounded by familiar smells and the stillness of a spring night, a vast sense of contentment carries me to sleep.

ISBN 1-41205996-8